WORKS 2000

in e

STEPHEN COPESTAKE

in easy steps is an imprint of Computer Step
Southfield Road . Southam
Warwickshire CV47 OFB . England

www.ineasysteps.com

Notice of Liability

Every effort has been made to ensure that this book contains accurate and current
information. However, Computer Step and the author shall not be liable for any loss or
damage suffered by readers as a result of any information contained herein.

Trademarks

Microsoft® and Windows® are registered trademarks of Microsoft Corporation. All
other trademarks are acknowledged as belonging to their respective companies.

Printed and bound in the United Kingdom

ISBN 1-84078-046-0

Table Of Contents

1

A common approach   7

Introduction   8
The Works 2000 toolbars   10
New document creation   11
Creating blank documents   12
Using Wizards   13
Creating your own templates   15
Using your templates   16
Opening Works 2000 documents   17
Saving Works 2000 documents   19
Sending documents via email   20
Using HELP Contents   21
Using HELP Index   22
Using the Answer Wizard   23
Other ways to get assistance   24

2

The Word Processor   25

The Word Processor screen   26
Entering text   27
Moving around in documents   28
Viewing special characters   30
Inserting special characters   31
Changing zoom levels   32
Formatting text – an overview   34
Changing the font and/or type size   35
Changing text colour   36
Changing the font style   37
Font effects   38
Indenting paragraphs – an overview   39
Applying indents to paragraphs   40
Aligning paragraphs   41
Specifying paragraph spacing   42
Line spacing – an overview   43
Adjusting line spacing   44
Working with columns   45
Paragraph borders   46
Paragraph fills   47
Working with tabs   48
Searching for text   50
Replacing text   51

Working with headers and footers 52
Inserting headers 53
Inserting footers 54
Amending headers and footers 55
Undoing actions 56
Redoing actions 57
Spell-checking 58
Grammar-checking 60
Searching for synonyms 61
Working with images 62
Brief notes on image formats 63
Inserting images – an overview 64
Inserting clip art 66
Inserting pictures 68
Gallery housekeeping 70
Using keywords 74
Searching for keywords 75
Importing clip art into the Gallery 76
Manipulating images – an overview 77
Rescaling images 78
Bordering images 80
Moving images 81
Wrapping text around images 82
Page setup – an overview 84
Specifying margins 85
Specifying the page size 86
Using Print Preview 88
Zooming in or out in Print Preview 89
Changing pages in Print Preview 90
Printer setup 91
Printing – an overview 92
Customised printing 93
Printing – the fast track approach 94

The Spreadsheet   95

3

The Spreadsheet screen 96
Entering data 97
Modifying existing data 99
Working with cell ranges 100
Moving around in spreadsheets 101
Changing Zoom levels 103
Selection techniques 105
Formulas – an overview 107
Inserting a formula 108
Functions – an overview 109

Using Easy Calc   110
Cell protection   111
Amending row/column sizes   113
Inserting rows or columns   114
Working with fills   115
Using AutoFill   116
Working with headers   117
Working with footers   118
Changing number formats   119
Changing fonts and styles   120
Cell alignment   121
Bordering cells   123
Shading cells   124
AutoFormat   125
Find operations   126
Search-and-replace operations   127
Charting – an overview   128
Creating a chart   129
Amending chart formats   130
Reformatting charts   131
Chart housekeeping   132
Page setup – an overview   133
Setting size/orientation options   134
Setting margin options   135
Other page setup options   136
Page setup for charts   137
Using Print Preview   138
Zooming in or out in Print Preview   139
Changing pages in Print Preview   140
Printing spreadsheet data   141
Printing – the fast track approach   142

The Database   143

4

The Database screen   144
Creating your first database   145
Entering data   146
Modifying existing data   148
Using Database views   149
Moving around in databases   151
Using Zoom   153
Selection techniques in List view   154
Selection techniques in forms   155
Formulas – an overview   156
Inserting a formula   157
Database functions   158

Inserting a function   159
Inserting fields   160
Inserting records   161
Amending record/field sizes   162
Working with fills   163
Working with fill series   164
Changing fonts and styles   165
Aligning field contents   166
Bordering fields   167
Shading fields   168
Find operations   169
Search-and-replace operations   170
Page setup – an overview   171
Setting size/orientation options   172
Setting margin options   173
Other page setup options   174
Report creation   175
Using Print Preview   176
Zooming in or out in Print Preview   177
Changing pages in Print Preview   178
Printing database data   179

The Calendar   181

5

The Calendar – an overview   182
The Calendar screen   183
Entering appointments   184
Appointment management   185
Entering events   186

Index   187

A common approach

This chapter shows you how Works 2000 provides a common look, so you can get started quickly in any module. You'll learn how to create new documents and open/save existing ones. You'll also learn how to send Works 2000 documents as email attachments, directly from within Works itself. Finally, you'll get information you need from Works 2000's online HELP system.

Covers

Introduction | 8

The Works 2000 toolbars | 10

New document creation | 11

Creating blank documents | 12

Using Wizards | 13

Creating your own templates | 15

Using your templates | 16

Opening Works 2000 documents | 17

Saving Works 2000 documents | 19

Sending documents via email | 20

Using HELP Contents | 21

Using HELP Index | 22

Using the Answer Wizard | 23

Other ways to get assistance | 24

Chapter One

Introduction

Works 2000 consists of four modules:

- The Word Processor

- The Spreadsheet

- The Database

- The Calendar

If you're using Works Suite 2000 instead of Works 2000, you won't have access to the Works Word Processor module. Instead, Word 2000 (Office 2000's full-featured word processor) will be installed.

(For how to use Word 2000, see 'Word 2000 in easy steps'.)

In a sense, the first three are 'cutdown' versions of Microsoft Word, Excel and Access. In spite of this, however, all the modules provide a high level of functionality and ease of use.

Another great advantage of Works 2000 is that it integrates the modules well. With the exception of the Calendar, they share a common look and feel.

The illustration below shows the Word Processor opening screen. Flagged are components which are common to the other modules, too (except Calendar).

Toolbar contents vary somewhat from module to module.

The ruler is only present in the Word Processor module.

Title bar   Menu bar

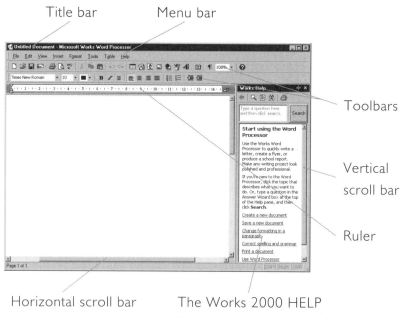

Toolbars

Vertical scroll bar

Ruler

Horizontal scroll bar

The Works 2000 HELP feature – see pages 21-24

Compare the Word Processor screen on the facing page with the following:

The Calendar's screen is rather different – see Chapter 5.

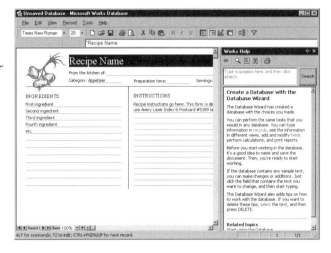

Database screen

There are, of course, differences between the module screens; we'll explore these in later chapters.

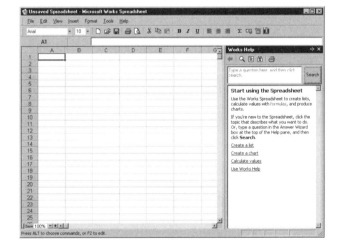

Spreadsheet screen

Notice that many of the screen components are held in common. The purpose of this shared approach is to ensure that users of Works 2000 can move between modules with the minimum of readjustment.

The Works 2000 toolbars

Toolbars are an important component in all of the Works 2000 modules. A toolbar is an on-screen bar which contains shortcut buttons. These symbolise (and allow easy access to) often used commands which would normally have to be invoked via one or more menus.

For example, the Word Processor's Standard and Formatting toolbars let you:

In the Spreadsheet, Database and Calendar modules, there is only one available toolbar.

- create, open, save and print documents

- perform copy-and-paste and cut-and-paste operations

- align, embolden, italicise or underline text

- apply a new typeface and/or type size to text

- spell- and grammar-check text

- send documents as email attachments

by simply clicking on the relevant button.

Toolbars vary to some extent from module to module.

Hiding/revealing toolbars

In the Database and Spreadsheet modules, pull down the View menu and click Toolbar to hide or reveal the toolbar, as appropriate.
In the Calendar, click Toolbar in the View menu. In the sub-menu, select Show Toolbar to hide or reveal the toolbar, as appropriate.

In the Word Processor, pull down the View menu and do the following:

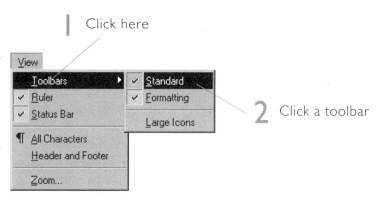

Click here

2 Click a toolbar

Re step 2 – the tick signifies that a toolbar is currently visible.

New document creation

Because the Word Processor, Database and Spreadsheet modules are uniform in the way they create new documents, we'll look at this topic here rather than in later module-specific chapters.

All Works 2000 modules (with the exception of Calendar) let you:

- create new blank documents

- create new documents with the help of a 'Wizard'

- create new documents based on a 'template' you've created yourself

Creating blank documents is the simplest route to new document creation; use this if you want to define the document components yourself from scratch. This is often not the most efficient way to create new documents.

Wizards are a shortcut to the creation of new documents. You work through one or more dialogs (usually one), answering the appropriate questions and making the relevant choices. Wizards greatly simplify and speed up the creation of new documents while at the same time producing highly professional results.

Templates are sample documents complete with the relevant formatting and/or text. When you've created and formatted a document (so that it meets your requirements) you can save it to disk as a template. Basing a new document on this template automatically provides access to any inherent text and/or formatting, a great timesaver.

Documents created with the use of Wizards or templates can easily be amended subsequently.

All three document creation methods involve launching the Works 2000 Task Launcher. This is a useful Internet-style screen which you can also use to open existing Works documents

For more information on opening Works documents, see page 17.

Creating blank documents

You can use a keyboard shortcut (but not in the Word Processor or Calendar) to run the Task Launcher. Simply press Ctrl+N.

You can create a new blank document from within any of the Works 2000 modules (except Calendar).

The first step is to launch the Task Launcher. From within any module except Calendar, pull down the File menu and click New. Now do the following:

To launch the Task Launcher from within Calendar, hold down Alt then press Tab until the Launcher's icon:

is visible in the on-screen bar. When it is, release Alt. (You can also use this technique in any other module.)

| Click Programs

2 Click the relevant module entry

If you've selected Works Database in step 1 (to create a new blank database), Works 2000 doesn't immediately comply after step 3; before it can do so, you need to define the necessary fields. (See page 145 for how to do this.)

3 Click Start a blank...

Running the Task Launcher automatically

If you want to create a new blank document immediately after you've started Works 2000, you don't need to launch the Task Launcher manually: it appears automatically.

Re step 3 – the text of the command varies according to module.

Once the Task Launcher is on-screen, however, you can follow the above steps to produce the relevant blank document.

Using Wizards

Works 2000 provides a large number of Wizards, organised under overall category headings. With these, you can create a wide variety of professional-quality documents (Works 2000 calls this carrying out tasks). For example, you can create recipe books, home inventories, fax cover sheets, brochures, flyers, menus, newsletters, school reports, invitations, student schedules, errand lists, graph paper, financial worksheets . . .

Basing new documents on a Wizard

In any Works 2000 modules except Calendar, pull down the File menu and click New. The Task Launcher appears. Carry out the following steps:

1 Select Tasks   3 Select a task

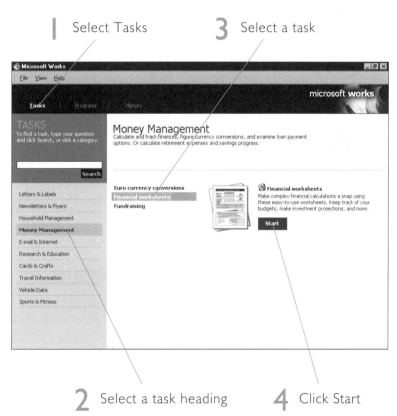

2 Select a task heading   4 Click Start

When you've selected the Wizard you want to use, Works 2000 launches a dialog which varies accordingly. However, the basic format is the same. Works is asking you to supply it with the information required by making the relevant choices.

Carry out the following steps:

5 Make the relevant choice

The equivalent dialog in other Wizards will be slightly different.

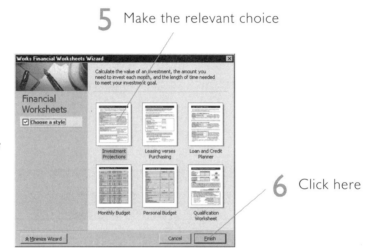

6 Click here

The end result:

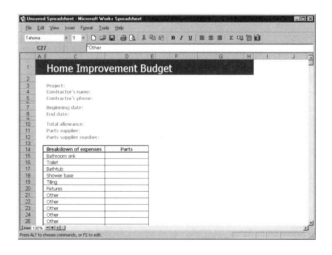

Here, a Budget spreadsheet has been created

Creating your own templates

To use a template you've created, follow the procedures on page 16.

In any Works 2000 module apart from Calendar, you can save an existing document (complete with all text and formatting) as a template. You can then use this template as the basis for new document creation. The text/formatting is immediately carried across.

Saving your work as a template

First, open the document you want to save as a template (for how to do this, see the 'Opening Works 2000 documents' topic later). Pull down the File menu and click Save As. Now do the following:

1 Click here. In the drop-down list, click the drive you want to host the template

Re step 2 – you may have to double-click one or more folders first, to locate the folder you want to host the new template.

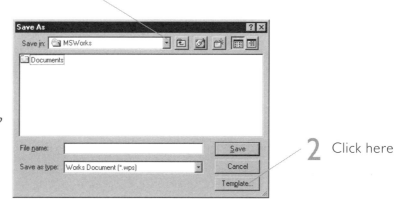

2 Click here

4 Click here

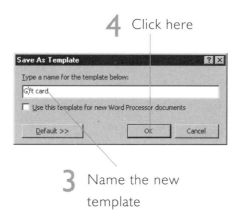

3 Name the new template

Using your templates

Any templates you create are automatically accessible from the Task Launcher under the heading 'Personal Templates'.

Opening a template

In the Task Launcher (either when you've just started Works 2000 or after you've started the Launcher manually), carry out the following steps:

1 Select Tasks   3 Select a template

2 Select Personal Templates   4 Click Start

Opening Works 2000 documents

We saw earlier that Works 2000 lets you create new documents in various ways. You can also open Word Processor, Spreadsheet and Database documents you've already created:

You can also use the Documents section of the Windows Startup menu to open recently used Works files – see your Windows documentation for how to do this.

- just after you've started Works 2000

- from within the relevant Works 2000 module

Opening an existing document at startup

Immediately after you've started Works, carry out steps 1 and 2:

Click History   Column headings

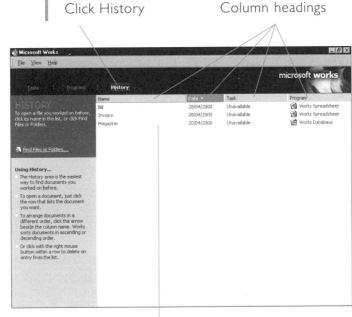

To view entries in a different order, click a column heading. Now do the following:

Click here to switch from Ascending to Descending view (or vice versa)

As an example, to sort items alphabetically by program module, click the Program heading. Then click the arrow to select Ascending or Descending as the sort order.

2 Click the row which represents the file you want to open

Opening a document from within a module

From within any Works 2000 module except Calendar, pull down the File menu and click Open. Now carry out the following steps, as appropriate:

You can use a keyboard shortcut to launch the Open dialog: simply press Ctrl+O.

2 Click here. In the drop-down list, click the drive which hosts the file

Re step 3 – you may have to double-click one or more folders first, to locate the file you want to open.

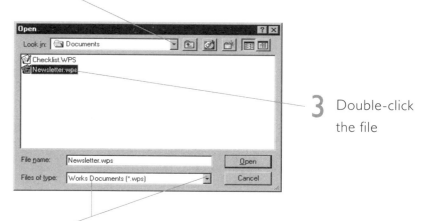

3 Double-click the file

I Make sure Works Documents... is shown here. If it isn't, click the arrow and select it in the list

You can open documents created in formats native to other programs into any Works 2000 module (this is called 'importing'). For example, you can import HTML or Word for Windows files (but note that any features which aren't found in Works are ignored).

In step 1, select the external format. Then follow steps 2-3.

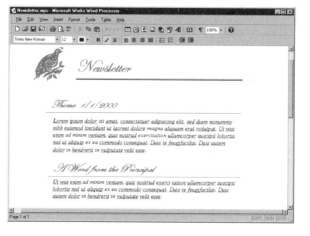

The opened newsletter

Saving Works 2000 documents

It's important to save your work at frequent intervals, in order to avoid data loss in the event of a hardware fault or power interruption. With the exception of the Calendar (which saves work automatically), Works 2000 uses a consistent approach to saving throughout its modules.

You can save Works 2000 documents in formats which can be utilised by other programs (this is called 'exporting'). For example, you can save files created in the Word Processor module into Word for Windows format, and then open (and edit) them there. Alternatively, you can save them into HTML format, for use on the World Wide Web.

After step 1, click in the Save as type: field. In the drop-down list, select the external format. Then follow steps 2-3.

Saving a document for the first time

In the Word Processor, Spreadsheet or Database modules, pull down the File menu and click Save. Or press Ctrl+S. Now do the following:

Click here. In the drop-down list, click the drive you want to host the file

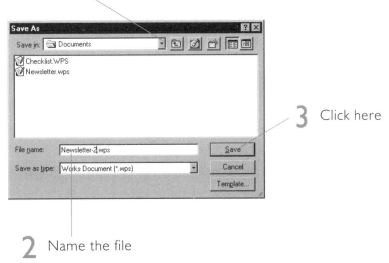

3 Click here

2 Name the file

Re step 2 – you may have to double-click one or more folders first, to locate the folder you want to host the new file.

Saving previously saved documents

In any of the modules apart from Calendar, pull down the File menu and click Save. Or press Ctrl+S. No dialog launches; instead, Works 2000 saves the latest version of your document to disk, overwriting the previous version.

Sending documents via email

You can send any Works 2000 file as an email attachment. When you do this, Works launches a new message in your email program – the Works document is automatically attached.

Emailing a Works 2000 file

Within any Works module, pull down the File menu and do the following:

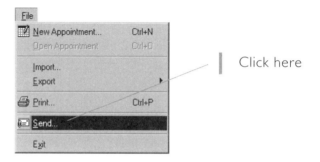

Click here

2 Complete any dialog which launches (in Calendar, select a style and date range), then click OK

Here, Outlook Express is being used to send a Works 2000 calendar as an attachment.

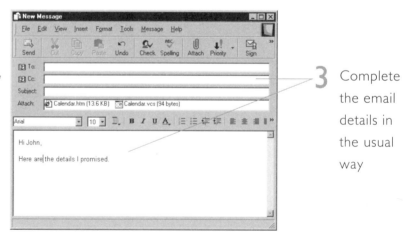

3 Complete the email details in the usual way

4 Complete any further options as necessary, then click Send

Using HELP Contents

Works 2000 has comprehensive Help facilities, organised under two broad headings:

- Contents (a list of program-specific topics)

- Index (an alphabetical list of topics)

To generate the Help Contents dialog from within any module (or the Task Launcher), pull down the Help menu and choose Contents.

Using Contents

Do the following:

You can use a keyboard shortcut to launch Help: simply press

F1.

Click this icon:

under the Title bar to launch Contents.

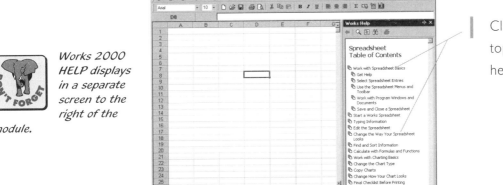

Click a topic heading

Works 2000 HELP displays in a separate screen to the right of the

module.

To print out HELP information, click this button immediately below the Title bar:

Complete the Print dialog, then click OK.

After step 1, Works 2000 launches a series of subheadings. Click one, then select a subsidiary topic (prefixed by 🗋 instead of 🗐). Works 2000 displays the topic in the HELP window.

2 When you've finished viewing the topic, click this button: ❌ in the upper right hand corner of the Contents window to close it

Using HELP Index

To generate the Help Index dialog from within any module (or the Task Launcher), pull down the Help menu and choose Index.

Using Index

Do the following:

You can use a keyboard shortcut to launch Help: simply press F1.

Click this icon:

under the Title bar to launch Index.

If typing in a keyword in step 1 does not produce a relevant topic, scroll through available headings here until you locate the right one, then double-click it and omit step 2.

(If you still can't find the correct heading, follow the procedures on page 23.)

1 Type in the word you want to look up

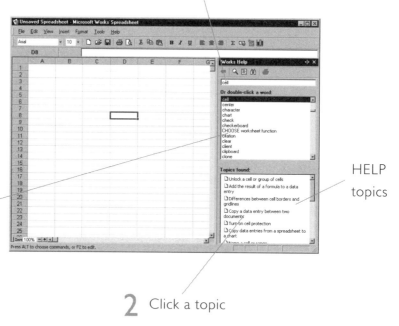

HELP topics

2 Click a topic

View the relevant topic. Finally, carry out step 3:

3 When you've finished viewing the topic, click this button: **X** in the upper right hand corner of the Index window to close it

To print out HELP information, click this button immediately below the Title bar:

Complete the Print dialog, then click OK.

Using the Answer Wizard

In any HELP window, click any link (coloured green) to display further information.

In the example below, the highlighted word 'scrolling' is clicked (Before); the result is a useful definition (After).

If neither of the methods on pages 21-22 works, you can use another. You can type in Plain English questions. When you've done this, you can have Works search through its HELP database for relevant topics.

Asking questions with the Answer Wizard

From within any HELP screen, do the following:

1 If the Answer Wizard isn't already displaying, click this button just below the HELP screen's Title bar:

Move around in a document
You can move around in a document by scrolling or by using the keys on the keyboard.

Before

Move around in a document
You can move around in a document by scrolling (with the mouse pointer, move quickly through a document by clicking the vertical bar at the right of a window or the horizontal bar at the bottom of a window) or by using the keys on the keyboard.

After

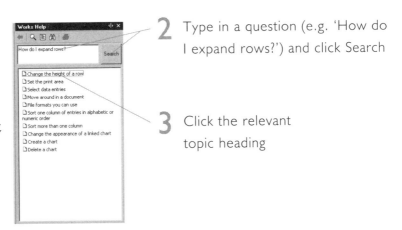

2 Type in a question (e.g. 'How do I expand rows?') and click Search

To close the Answer Wizard, follow step 3 on page 22.

3 Click the relevant topic heading

To print out HELP information, click this button immediately below the Title bar:

Complete the Print dialog, then click OK.

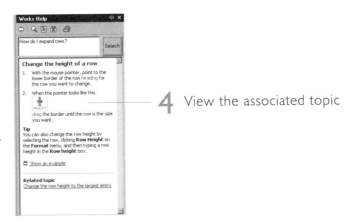

4 View the associated topic

Other ways to get assistance

There are more immediate ways to get help:

Works 2000 calls these highly specific HELP bubbles 'ToolTips'.

- moving the mouse pointer over Toolbar buttons produces an explanatory HELP bubble:

- Fields in dialogs have associated Help boxes. To view a box, first right-click in a field. Then carry out the following procedure:

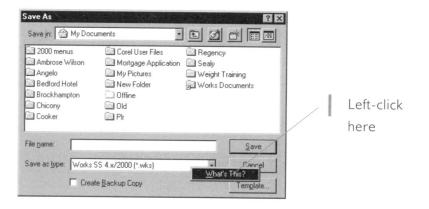

Left-click here

2 Works 2000 now launches a HELP box:

When you've finished with a Help box, press Esc to close it.

Specifies the type of file you are saving.

Other standard Windows HELP features are also present; see your Windows documentation for how to use these.

The Word Processor

This chapter gives you the basics of using the Word Processor. You'll learn how to negotiate the screen (also with Zoom), enter/proof text and perform find-and-replace operations. You'll also discover how to format and align text (including the use of headers/footers), and then undo/redo editing actions. Finally, you'll learn how to insert clip art with the Clip Gallery and third-party pictures via a dialog route, and then customise page layout/printing.

Covers

The Word Processor screen | 26

Entering text | 27

Moving around in documents | 28

Working with special characters | 30

Changing zoom levels | 32

Formatting text | 34

Searching for and replacing text | 50

Headers and footers | 52

Undo and Redo | 56

Text proofing | 58

Working with images (clip art and pictures) | 62

Page setup and printing | 84

Chapter Two

The Word Processor screen

Below is an illustration of the Word Processor screen.

Title bar   Menu bar

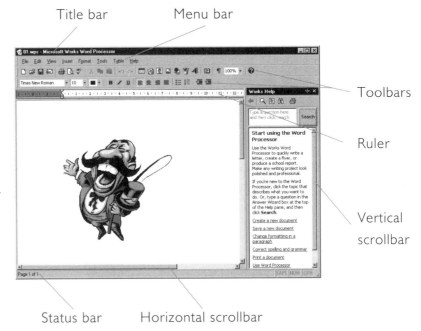

Toolbars

Ruler

Vertical scrollbar

The Status bar displays information relating to the active document (e.g. what page you're on, and the total number of pages).

Status bar   Horizontal scrollbar

Some of these – e.g. the ruler and scrollbars – are standard to just about all programs which run under Windows. A few of them can be hidden, if required.

Specifying which screen components display

Pull down the View menu. Then perform steps 1-2 to view/hide toolbars (or follow the procedures in the HOT TIP).

To view or hide the Ruler or Status bar, click Ruler or Status bar in step 1, then omit step 2.

Re step 2 – the tick signifies that a toolbar is currently visible.

Click here

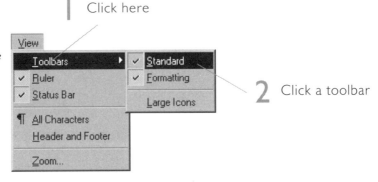

Click a toolbar

Entering text

The Word Processor lets you enter text immediately after you've started it. You enter text at the insertion point:

The Word Processor has automatic word wrap. This means that you don't have to press Return to enter text on a new line: a new line is automatically started for you, when required.

Only press Return if you need to begin a new paragraph.

A magnified view of the text insertion point

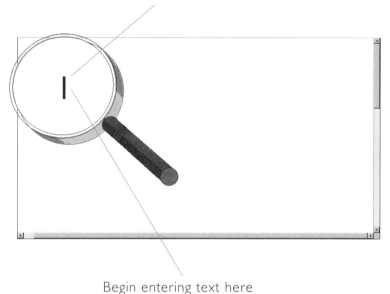

Begin entering text here

To word-count specific paragraphs, pre-select them. Then perform step 1.

Performing a word count

Writers (in particular) find it useful to be able to perform a word count.

After step 1, the Word Processor launches a special message. Do the following:

Pull down the Tools menu and do the following:

Click here

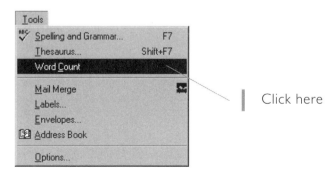

Click here

Moving around in documents

You can use the following to move through Word Processor documents:

- keystrokes

- the vertical/horizontal scrollbars

- the Find and Replace dialog

Using keystrokes

Works 2000 implements the standard Windows direction keys. Use the left, right, up and down cursor keys in the usual way. Additionally, Home, End, Page Up and Page Down work normally.

Using the scrollbars

Use your mouse to perform any of the following actions;

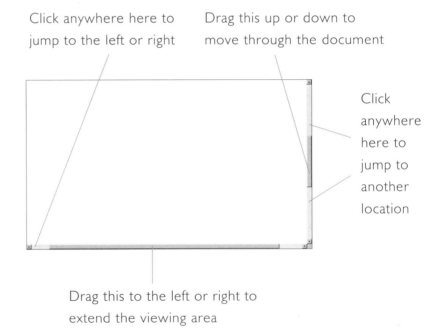

Click anywhere here to jump to the left or right

Drag this up or down to move through the document

Click anywhere here to jump to another location

Drag this to the left or right to extend the viewing area

Using the Find and Replace dialog

You can use the Find and Replace dialog to move to any page number within the open document.

Pull down the Edit menu and click Go To. Now do the following:

You can use a keyboard shortcut to launch the relevant incarnation of the Find and Replace dialog. Simply press Ctrl+G.

Ensure Page is selected, then type in a page number

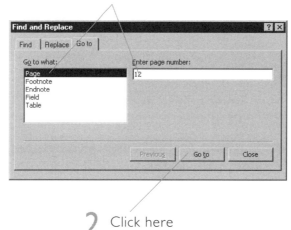

2 Click here

To insert a footnote or endnote into a document, place the insertion point at the relevant location. Pull down the Insert menu and click Footnote. In the dialog which launches, select Footnote or Endnote. Click OK. Finally, type in the note text then return to the body of the document.

You can also use the Find and Replace dialog to move to pre-inserted footnotes or endnotes. Footnotes are references or notes placed at the bottom of the page, while endnotes are positioned at the end of the relevant document (or – less commonly – at the end of sections). Footnotes and endnotes are prefaced with numbers. For how to insert footnotes/endnotes, see the HOT TIP.

Once you've inserted an endnote or footnote, you can then have the Word Processor jump to it.

Launch the Find and Replace dialog, as above. In step 1, select Footnote or Endnote and type in the note number. Then carry out step 2.

Viewing special characters

The Word Processor has a special view mode whereby special characters:

- manual hyphens

- non-breaking spaces

- paragraph marks

- spaces

can be made visible. This is sometimes useful. For example, if you want to ensure there are no double spaces between words (something which happens surprisingly often), it's much easier to delete the unwanted spaces if you can see them.

You can insert the Euro symbol into Word Processor documents. **Fonts which support this include:**

- *Arial*
- *Courier New*
- *Impact*
- *Tahoma, and;*
- *Times New Roman*

To insert the Euro symbol, press the Num Lock key on your keyboard. Hold down Alt and press 0128 (consecutively). Release Alt and turn off Num Lock.

Viewing hidden characters
Pull down the View menu and click All Characters.

The illustration below shows a magnified view of 3 (normally invisible) characters:

An inserted
Euro symbol

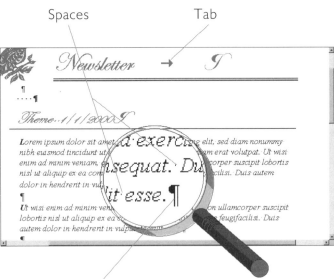

Spaces   Tab

Paragraph mark symbol

Inserting special characters

To insert special (hidden) characters, carry out the following procedure.

Inserting hidden characters

Pull down the Insert menu and do the following:

One effect of justifying text (see page 41) is that Works 2000 increases the gaps between words to ensure that the text meets both the left and right margins. This can result in unsightly results (especially in columns).

You can combat this by inserting a manual hyphen into a troublesome word. Doing so forces part of the word onto the next line, making the text visually more attractive. However, if you later insert additional text or delete existing text (so that the original problem no longer applies and the word appears on another line), the hyphen disappears.

To insert a manual hyphen, click anywhere in the relevant word. Follow steps 1-2. In step 3, select Optional Hyphen. Perform step 4.

Click here

2 Select this tab

3 Double-click a character

4 Click here

Changing zoom levels

The ability to vary the level of magnification for the active document is often useful. Sometimes, it's helpful to 'zoom out' (i.e. decrease the magnification) so that you can take an overview; at other times, you'll need to 'zoom in' (increase the magnification) to work in greater detail.

The Word Processor module lets you do either of these very easily.

You can do any of the following:

• choose from preset zoom levels (e.g. 100%, 75%)

• specify your own zoom percentage

• choose a zoom setting based on document margins

Setting the zoom level

Pull down the View menu and do the following:

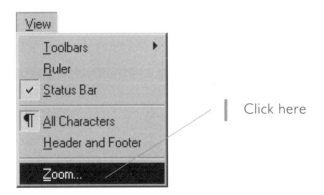

Click here

2 Follow step 3, 4 OR 5 on the facing page. Finally, carry out step 6

3 Click a preset zoom level

*Re step 5 –
entries here
must lie in the
following range:
25%-500%*

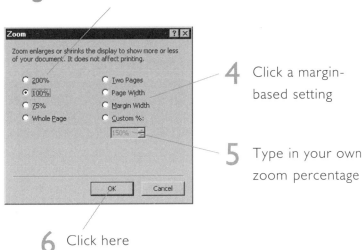

4 Click a margin-
based setting

5 Type in your own
zoom percentage

6 Click here

Zoom set
to 75%

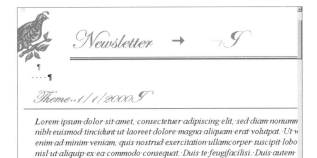

Zoom set
to 150%

Formatting text – an overview

The Word Processor lets you format text in a variety of ways. Very broadly, however, and for the sake of convenience, text formatting can be divided into two overall categories:

Character formatting

Character formatting is concerned with altering the *appearance* of selected text. Examples include:

- changing the font

- changing the type size

- colouring text

- changing the font style (bold, italic, underlining etc.)

- applying font effects (e.g. superscript/subscript, outline and shadow)

Character formatting is a misnomer in one sense: it can also be applied to specified paragraphs of text, or to parts of specified paragraphs.

Paragraph formatting

Paragraph formatting has to do with the structuring and layout of paragraphs of text. Examples include:

- specifying paragraph indents

- specifying paragraph alignment (e.g. left or right justification)

- specifying paragraph and line spacing

- imposing borders and/or fills on paragraphs

Changing the font and/or type size

Character formatting can be changed in two ways:

- from within the Font dialog

- (to a lesser extent) by using the Formatting toolbar

 The Word Processor uses standard Windows procedures for text selection.

Applying a new font or type size (1)

First, select the text whose typeface and/or type size you want to amend. Pull down the Format menu and click Font. Now carry out steps 1 and/or 2 below. Finally, follow step 3:

 Re step 1 – as well as whole point sizes, you can also enter half-point increments; i.e. the Word Processor will accept:

10, 10.5 or 11

but not:

10.75 or 11.2

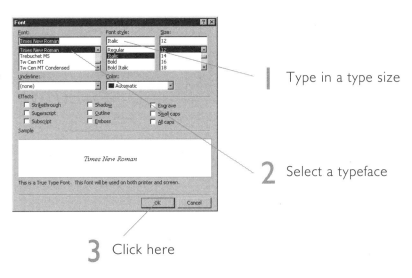

1 Type in a type size

2 Select a typeface

3 Click here

Applying a new font or type size (2)

Make sure the Formatting toolbar is visible. Now select the text you want to amend and do the following:

 If the Formatting toolbar isn't currently visible, pull down the View menu and click Toolbars, Formatting.

Click here; select the font you want to use in the drop-down list

Type in the type size you need and press Enter

Changing text colour

You can change the colour of text by using the Font dialog, or via the Formatting toolbar.

Colouring text (1)

First, select the text you want to alter. Pull down the Format dialog and click Font. Now do the following:

Click here; in the list which launches, select a colour

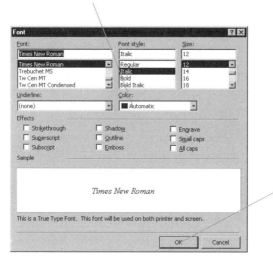

2 Click here

Re step 1 – selecting Automatic in the colour list sets the colour to black (unless you've amended the default Windows text colour).

Colouring text (2)

Make sure the Formatting toolbar is visible. Now select the text you want to amend and do the following:

Click here; in the list which launches, select a colour

Changing the font style

In the Word Processor, the following styles are available:

- Bold

- *Italic*

- <u>Underline</u>

You can use the Font dialog or the Toolbar to change styles.

Amending the font style (1)

First, select the text whose style you want to change. Then pull down the Format menu and click Font. Perform steps 1-2:

You can also use the following keyboard shortcuts:

Ctrl+B	*Emboldens text*
Ctrl+I	*Italicises text*
Ctrl+U	*Underlines text*

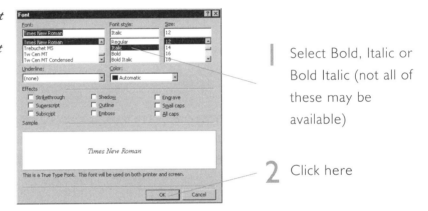

Select Bold, Italic or Bold Italic (not all of these may be available)

2 Click here

Amending the font style (2)

First, select the relevant text. Ensure the Formatting toolbar is visible. Then carry out any of the following:

If the Formatting toolbar isn't currently visible, pull down the View menu and click Toolbars, Formatting.

Click here for Bold

Click here for Underline

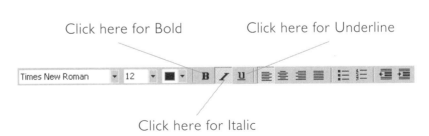

Click here for Italic

Font effects

You can also use the following keyboard shortcuts:

Ctrl++   *Superscript*
Ctrl+=   *Subscript*

Re step 1 – you can also use the dialog route to apply additional effects:

• *Shadow*
• *Outline*
• *Emboss, and;*
• *Engrave*

You can use the following font effects in Word Processor documents:

• Superscript – e.g. f$^{\text{ont effect}}$

• Subscript – e.g. f$_{\text{ont effect}}$

• ~~Strikethrough~~

• SMALL CAPS

• ALL CAPS

Applying font effects

First, select the relevant text. Pull down the Format dialog and click Font. Then carry out the following steps:

Apply one or more effects

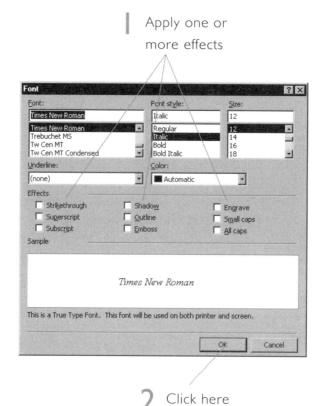

2 Click here

Indenting paragraphs – an overview

You can achieve a similar effect by using tabs. However, indents are easier to apply (and amend subsequently).

Indents are a crucial component of document layout. For instance, in most document types indenting the first line of paragraphs (i.e. moving it inwards away from the left page margin) makes the text much more legible.

Other document types – e.g. bibliographies – can use the following:

- hanging indents (where the first line is unaltered, while subsequent lines are indented)

- full indents (where the entire paragraph is indented away from the left and/or the right margins)

Some of the potential indent combinations are shown in the illustration below:

Don't confuse indents with page margins. Margins are the gap between the edge of the page and the text area; indents define the distance between the margins and text.

The Word Processor doesn't actually display margins: they've been inserted here for illustration purposes.

This paragraph has a full left and right indent. It's best, however, not to overdo the extent of the indent: 0.35 inches is often more than adequate.

Left and right ('full') indent

This paragraph has a first-line indent. This type of indent is suitable for most document types. It's best, however, not to overdo the extent of the indent: 0.35 inches is often more than adequate.

First-line indent

This paragraph has a hanging indent. It's best, however, not to overdo the extent of the indent: 0.35 inches is often more than adequate.

Hanging indent

Left margin   Right margin

Applying indents to paragraphs

Paragraphs can be indented from within the Paragraph dialog, or (to a lesser extent) by using the Formatting toolbar (if you add extra buttons to it).

Indenting text with the Font dialog

First, select the paragraph(s) you want to indent. Pull down the Format menu and click Paragraph. Now follow step 1 below. If you want a left indent, carry out step 2. For a right indent, follow step 3. To achieve a first-line or hanging indent, follow step 4. Finally, irrespective of the indent type, carry out step 5.

Ensure this tab is active

Re step 4 – to implement a hanging indent, type in a negative value (e.g. −0.35) and the equivalent value in the Left field (e.g. −0.35).

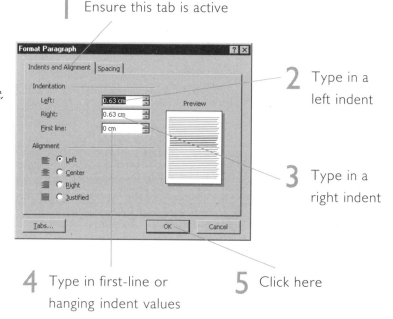

2 Type in a left indent

3 Type in a right indent

4 Type in first-line or hanging indent values

5 Click here

Using the Formatting toolbar to apply indents

Use these buttons in the Formatting toolbar:

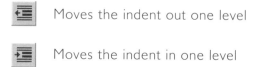

Moves the indent out one level

Moves the indent in one level

Aligning paragraphs

You can use the following types of alignment:

Left   Text is flush with the left page margin

Center   Text aligns equidistantly between the left and right page margins

Right   Text is flush with the right page margin

Justified   Text is flush with the left *and* right page margins

Aligning text with the Format Paragraph dialog

First, select the paragraph(s) you want to align. Pull down the Format menu and click Paragraph. Now:

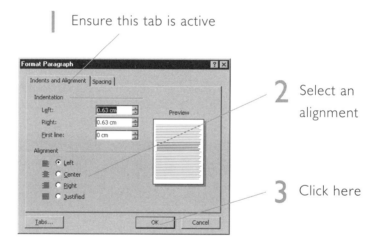

Ensure this tab is active

2 Select an alignment

3 Click here

Aligning text with the Formatting toolbar

Select the relevant paragraph(s). Then click any of these:

Left align   Right align

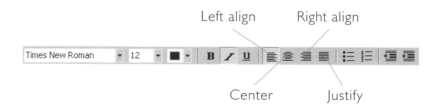

Center   Justify

Specifying paragraph spacing

As a general rule, set low paragraph spacing settings: a little goes a long way.

You can customise the vertical space before and/or after specific text paragraphs.

The Word Processor defines paragraph spacing in terms of whole lines.

Applying paragraph spacing

First, select the paragraph(s) whose spacing you want to adjust. Pull down the Format menu and carry out the steps below:

| Click here

2 Ensure the Spacing tab is active

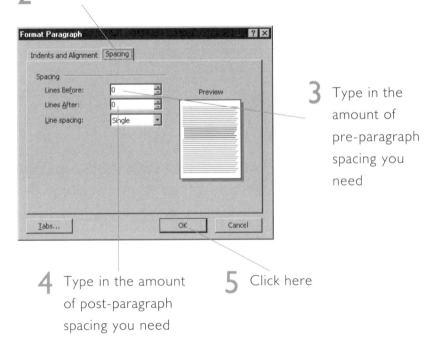

3 Type in the amount of pre-paragraph spacing you need

4 Type in the amount of post-paragraph spacing you need

5 Click here

Line spacing – an overview

It's often necessary to amend line spacing. This is the vertical distance between individual lines of text, or more accurately between the baseline (the imaginary line on which text appears to sit) of one line and the baseline of the previous.

Line spacing is also known as leading (pronounced 'ledding').

The Word Processor lets you apply the following line spacing settings:

- Single

- 1.5 Lines

- Double

- Triple

- Quadruple

The first three are the most commonly used:

You can use the following keyboard shortcuts to adjust line spacing:

Ctrl+1	*Single spacing*
Ctrl+5	*1 ½ spacing*
Ctrl+2	*Double spacing*
Ctrl+3	*Triple spacing*

This paragraph is in single line spacing. Newspapers frequently use this.

This paragraph is in 1½ line spacing. Probably no one uses this, but it serves as a useful illustration.

This paragraph is in double line spacing; writers use this when preparing manuscripts

Single line spacing

1.5 line spacing

Double line spacing

Adjusting line spacing

First, select the relevant paragraph(s). Then pull down the Format menu and do the following:

If you've just created a new document, you can set the line spacing before you begin to enter text.
Simply leave the insertion point at the start of the document and then follow the procedures outlined here.

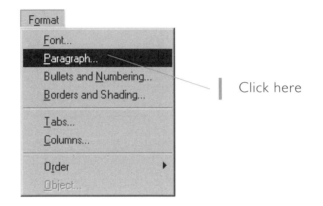

Click here

2 Ensure the Spacing tab is active

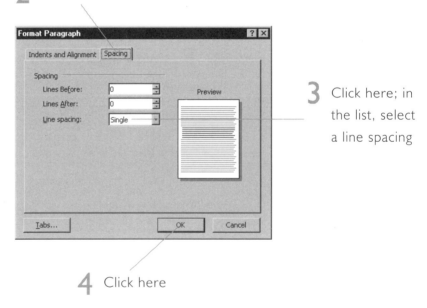

3 Click here; in the list, select a line spacing

4 Click here

Working with columns

The Word Processor module lets you arrange text into columns. You can:

- insert multiple columns

- specify the inter-column gap

- have Works insert a vertical line between columns

Applying columns

Place the insertion point anywhere within the current Word Processor document. Pull down the Format menu and do the following:

Works 2000 columns have certain (relative) restrictions.

Namely:

- *they apply to the entire document (not specific pages), and;*

- *they have the same width (calculated automatically by Works according to the left/right page margins and the inter-column gap)*

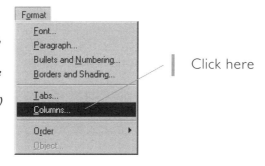
Click here

If you want the columns separated by lines, select this:

Re step 2 – the number of columns you can insert depends on:

- *your margin settings, and;*

- *the amount of inter-column gap*

2 Type in the no. of columns

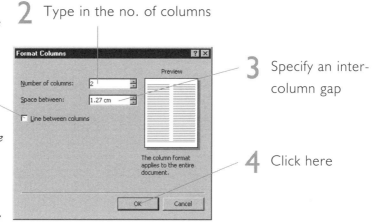

3 Specify an inter-column gap

4 Click here

Paragraph borders

By default, the Word Processor does not border paragraph text. However, you can apply a wide selection of borders if you want. You can specify:

- the border type/thickness

- how many sides the border should have (all four, or permutations of Left, Right, Top and Bottom)

- the border colour

Applying a border

First, select the paragraph(s) you want to border. Then pull down the Format menu and click Borders and Shading. Now do the following:

1 Ensure Paragraph is selected

2 Click here; select a border style

3 Select the extent of the border

Re step 3 – by default, Outline is selected. This means that all 4 sides are bordered. If you don't want this, deselect Outline then select one or more individual options (e.g. Left, or Top and Right).

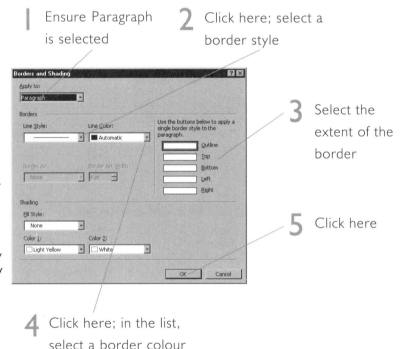

5 Click here

4 Click here; in the list, select a border colour

Paragraph fills

By default, the Word Processor does not apply a fill to text paragraphs. However, you can do the following if you want:

- apply a simple fill

- apply a simple pattern

- specify the foreground fill colour

- specify the background fill colour

Applying a fill

First, select the paragraph(s) you want to fill. Then pull down the Format menu and click Borders and Shading. Now carry out step 1 below. Follow steps 2, 3 and/or 4 as appropriate. Finally, carry out step 5:

1 Ensure Paragraph is selected

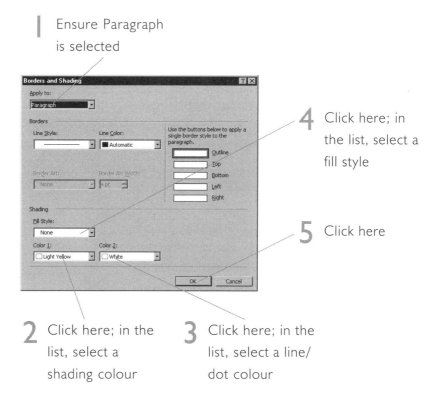

4 Click here; in the list, select a fill style

5 Click here

2 Click here; in the list, select a shading colour

3 Click here; in the list, select a line/ dot colour

Working with tabs

Tabs are a means of indenting the first line of text paragraphs (you can also use indents for this purpose – see pages 39-40).

When you press the Tab key while the text insertion point is at the start of a paragraph, the text in the first line jumps to the next tab stop:

This is a tab in action – for how to view the underlying tab mark, see page 30.

Lorem ipsum dolor sit amet, consectetuer adipiscing elit, sed diam nonummy nibh euismod tincidunt ut laoreet dolore magna aliquam erat volutpat. Ut wisi enim ad minim veniam, quis nostrud exercitation ullamcorper suscipit lobortis nisl ut aliquip ex ea commodo consequat. Duis te feugifacilisi. Duis autem dolor in hendrerit in vulputate velit esse.

This is a useful way to increase the legibility of your text.

By default, tab stops are inserted automatically every half an inch. If you want, however, you can enter new or revised tab stop positions individually.

Setting tab stops

Never use the Space Bar to indent paragraphs. The result of doing so is at best uneven, because spaces vary in size according to the typeface and type size applying to specific paragraphs.

First, select the paragraph(s) in which you need to set tab stops. Pull down the Format menu and do the following:

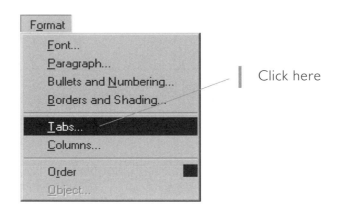

Click here

2 If existing individual tab stops are present (see the tip), carry out step 4 below.

3 If you want to implement a new default tab stop position, follow step 5. If, on the other hand, you need to set up individual tab stops, carry out steps 6-7 as often as necessary. Finally, in either case follow step 8 to confirm your changes.

6 Type in a single tab stop

7 Click here

When you've performed steps 6-7, the individual tab stop position appears here:

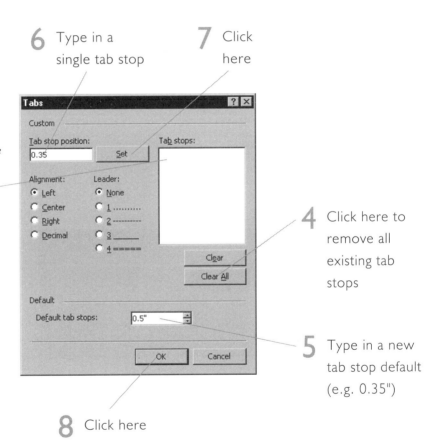

4 Click here to remove all existing tab stops

5 Type in a new tab stop default (e.g. 0.35")

8 Click here

Searching for text

You can search for specific text within the active document.

You can also search for special characters. For example, you can look for paragraph marks, tabs, wildcards, question marks, page breaks and spaces.

You can also:

- limit the search to words which match the case of the text you specify (e.g. if you search for 'Arm', Works 2000 will not flag 'arm' or 'ARM') – see step 2

- limit the search to whole words (e.g. if you search for 'eat', Works will not flag 'beat' or 'meat') – see step 2

Initiating a text search

Pull down the Edit menu and click Find. Carry out step 1. Perform steps 2 and 3-4 as appropriate. Finally, carry out step 5:

You can use a keyboard shortcut to launch the Find dialog. Simply press Ctrl+F.

The Word Processor has three wildcards (characters which can stand for others). These are:

Any Digit	*Stands for any number*
Any Letter	*Stands for any letter*
Any Character	*Stands for any number or letter*

Select any of these in step 4.

See pages 30-31 for more information on special characters.

Type in the text you want to find

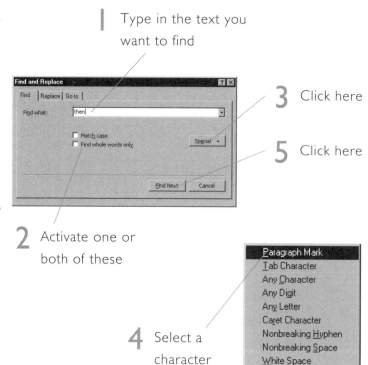

3 Click here

5 Click here

2 Activate one or both of these

4 Select a character

Replacing text

When you've located text, you can have the Word Processor replace it automatically with the text of your choice.

You can customise find-and-replace operations with the same parameters as a simple Find operation. For example, you can make them case-specific, or only replace whole words. You can also incorporate a variety of special characters.

You can use a keyboard shortcut here. Simply press Ctrl+H.

Re steps 4-5 – if you launch the special character menu after step 2, fewer options display. (For obvious reasons, wildcards are unavailable.)

If you don't want all instances of the text replaced automatically, don't carry out step 6. Instead, click the Find Next button after step 5. When the first match has been found, do one of the following:

• click Replace if you want it replaced, or;

• click Find Next again to leave it alone and locate the next match

Repeat this as often as necessary.

Initiating a find-and-replace operation

First pull down the Edit menu and click Replace. Follow step 1 and/or steps 4-5 (if appropriate). Carry out step 2 and/or steps 4-5 (if relevant). Perform step 3, if applicable. Finally, perform step 6 (or see the DON'T FORGET tip):

1 Type in the text you want to find

2 Type in the replacement text

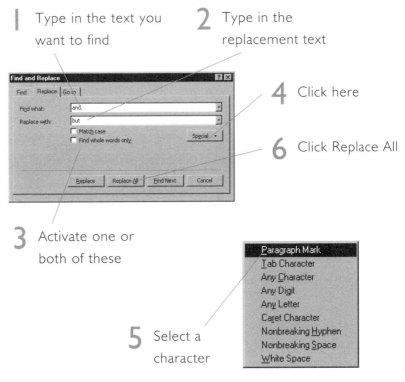

4 Click here

6 Click Replace All

3 Activate one or both of these

5 Select a character

Working with headers and footers

You can have the Word Processor print text at the top of each page within a document; the area of the page where repeated text appears is called the 'header'. In the same way, you can have text printed at the base of each page; in this case, the relevant page area is called the 'footer'.

Headers and footers are printed within the top and bottom page margins, respectively.

By default, the header and footer areas (but not the contents) are invisible.

Headers and footers in action:

Header

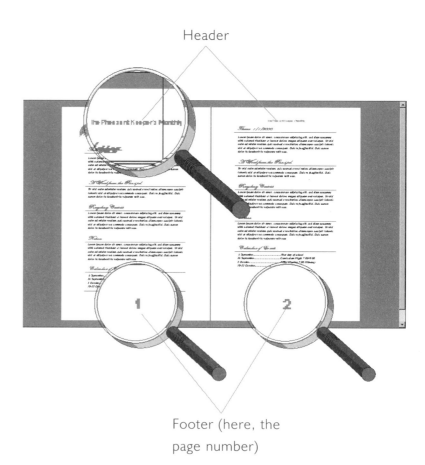

Footer (here, the
page number)

Inserting headers

Creating a header

To create a header, pull down the View menu and do the
following:

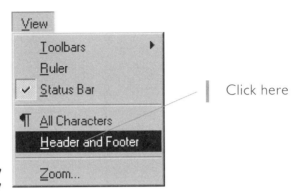

Click here

*Header text can
be formatted in
the normal
way. For
instance, you
can apply a new font and/or
type size.*

2 Enter – then format –
the relevant header text

The Header/
Footer toolbar

*Re step 2 –
you can have
the Word
Processor
insert a special
code which automatically
inserts the page number in
the header.*

  *To do this, click this
button:*

in the dedicated toolbar.

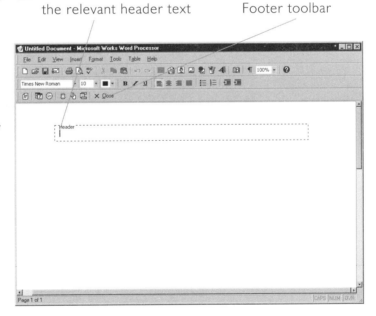

3 When you've finished, click this button: ☒ Close in the
dedicated toolbar

Inserting footers

Creating a footer

To create a footer, pull down the View menu and do the following:

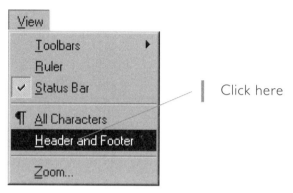

Click here

Footer text can be formatted in the normal way. For instance, you can apply a new font and/or type size.

2 Click this button: in the dedicated toolbar

3 Enter – then format – the relevant footer text

Re step 3 – you can have the Word Processor insert a special code which automatically inserts the page number in the footer.

To do this, click this button:

in the dedicated toolbar.

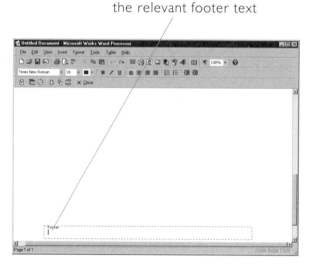

4 When you've finished, click this button: ✕ Close in the dedicated toolbar

Amending headers and footers

To amend existing header or footer text, do the following:

1   Carry out step 1 on the facing page.

2   If you want to amend a footer, carry out step 2 on the facing page

3   Perform step 4 and/or 5 below:

4   Amend the header text and/or formatting

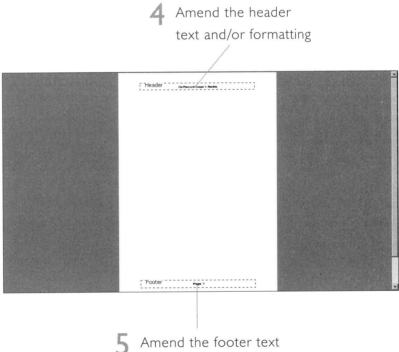

5   Amend the footer text and/or formatting

6   When you've finished, click this button: ✕ Close in the dedicated toolbar

Undoing actions

The Word Processor lets you reverse – 'undo' – just about any editing operation.

You can undo actions in the following ways (in descending order of complexity):

You can undo as many as 100 consecutive editing actions.

- via the keyboard

- from within the Edit menu

- from within the Standard toolbar

Using the keyboard

Simply press Ctrl+Z to undo an action. Repeat to perform consecutive undos.

Using the Edit menu

Pull down the Edit menu and do the following:

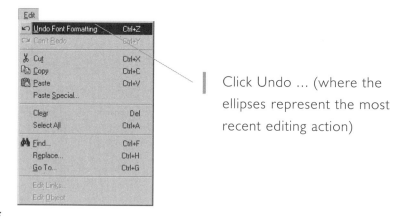

Click Undo ... (where the ellipses represent the most recent editing action)

Repeat step 1 for as many editing actions as you want to undo.

Using the Standard toolbar

Refer to the Standard toolbar and do the following as often as necessary:

Click here

Redoing actions

If, in the event, you decide that you *do* want to proceed with an operation which you've reversed, you can 'redo' it. In effect, this amounts to undoing an undo.

You can redo actions in the following ways (in descending order of complexity):

- via the keyboard

You can redo as many as 100 consecutive undos.

- from within the Edit menu

- from within the Standard toolbar

Using the keyboard

Simply press Ctrl+Y to undo an action.

Using the Edit menu

Pull down the Edit menu and do the following:

Repeat step 1 for as many editing actions as you want to redo.

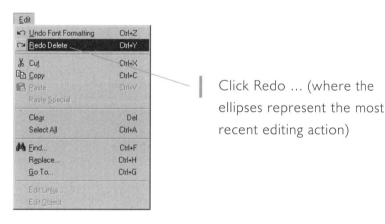

Click Redo ... (where the ellipses represent the most recent editing action)

Using the Standard toolbar

Refer to the Standard toolbar and do the following:

Click here

Spell-checking

The Word Processor lets you check text in two ways:

- on-the-fly, as you type in text

- separately, after the text has been entered

Checking text on-the-fly

This is the default. When automatic checking is in force, Works 2000 flags words it doesn't agree with, using a wavy red underline. If the word or phrase is wrong, right-click in it. Then carry out steps 1, 2 or 3:

1 Works 2000 often provides a list of alternatives. If one is correct, click it; the flagged word is replaced with the correct version

Re step 2 – when Works has flagged a word you have an extra option.

Click Add if:

- *the flagged word is correct, and;*

- *you want Works to remember it in future spell-checks, by adding it to your personal dictionary – see the DON'T FORGET tip on the facing page*

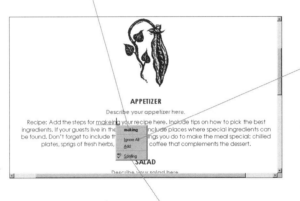

2 If you want the flagged word to stand, click Ignore All

3 If the flagged word is wrong but can't be corrected now, click Spelling and complete the resulting dialog – see the facing page

Disabling on-the-fly spell-checking

Pull down the Tools menu and click Options. Deselect Background spell checking. Click OK.

Works 2000 makes use of two separate dictionaries. One – called your personal dictionary – is yours. When you click the Add button (see the tip below and on the facing page), the flagged word is stored in your personal dictionary and recognised in future checking sessions.

Checking text separately

To check all the text within the active document in one go, pull down the Tools menu and click Spelling and Grammar. The Word Processor starts spell-checking the document from the text insertion point. When it encounters a word or phrase it doesn't recognise, Works 2000 flags it and produces a special dialog (see below). Usually, it provides alternative suggestions; if one of these is correct, you can opt to have it replace the flagged word. You can do this singly (i.e. just this instance is replaced) or globally (where all future instances – within the current checking session – are replaced).

Alternatively, you can have Works ignore *this* instance of the flagged word, ignore *all* future instances of the word or add the word to your personal dictionary (see the tips). After this, checking is resumed.

Carry out step 1 below, then follow step 2. Alternatively, carry out step 3 or 4 (or see the HOT TIP).

If you're correcting a spelling error, you have two further options:

- *click Add to have the flagged word stored in your personal dictionary (see above), or;*
- *click Change All to have Works substitute its suggestion for all future instances of the flagged word*

1 If one of the suggestions here is correct, click it, then follow step 2

3 Click here to ignore just this instance

4 Click here to ignore all future instances

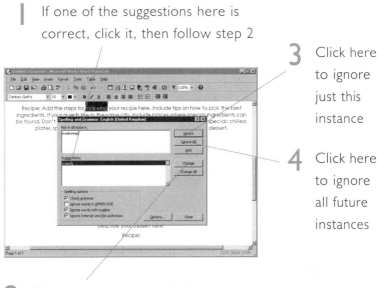

2 Click here to replace this instance

Grammar-checking

The less formal styles are less prone to query colloquialisms etc.

To apply a new writing style, launch the Spelling and Grammar dialog. Now click this button:

Options...

In the Options dialog, click in the Writing style: field. In the list, click a style. Click OK, then resume grammar-checking.

You can also have the Word Processor check a document's grammar (but only as a separate operation, not on-the-fly). It does this by applying collections of rules called 'writing styles'. There are four writing styles you can choose from:

- Casual

- Standard

- Formal

- Technical

Standard should be suitable for most purposes, but apply any of the rest as and when necessary (see the HOT TIP).

Grammar-checking text

Pull down the Tools menu and click Spelling and Grammar. Carry out step 1 below, then follow step 2. Alternatively, carry out step 3 or 4.

To disable grammar-checking (so that only spelling mistakes are flagged), launch the Options dialog (see the above tip). In the dialog, deselect Check grammar. Click OK.

1 If one of the suggestions here is correct, click it, then follow step 2

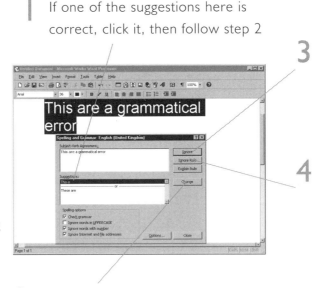

3 Click Ignore to ignore just this instance

4 Click Ignore Rule to ignore all future instances in this session

2 Click here to replace this instance

If you aren't sure about the grammatical rule currently being exercised, click this button for clarification:

Explain Rule

Read the message which appears, then click OK.

Searching for synonyms

The Word Processor lets you search for synonyms while you're editing the active document. You do this by calling up the resident Thesaurus. The Thesaurus categorises words into meanings, and each meaning is allocated various synonyms from which you can choose.

As a bonus, the Thesaurus also supplies:

- antonyms (e.g. if you look up 'good', Works lists 'poor')

- related words (e.g. if you look up 'author', Works lists 'critic')

You can also use a keyboard shortcut to launch the Thesaurus. Simply press Shift+F7.

Using the Thesaurus

First, select the word for which you require a synonym, antonym or related term. (Or simply position the insertion point within it). Pull down the Tools menu and click Thesaurus. Now do the following:

The selected word appears here

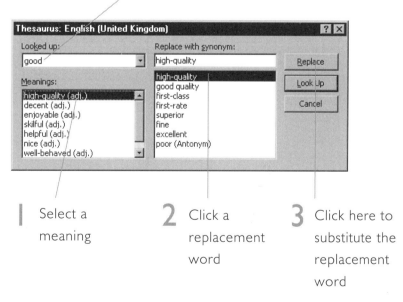

1 Select a meaning

2 Click a replacement word

3 Click here to substitute the replacement word

Working with images

The Word Processor module lets you add colour or greyscale images to the active document. Images – also called graphics – include:

- drawings produced in other programs

- clip art

- scanned photographs

Use images – whatever their source – to add much needed visual impact to documents. But use them judiciously: too much colour can be off-putting, and ultimately self-defeating.

Images are stored in various third-party formats. These formats are organised into two basic types:

Bitmap images

Bitmaps consist of pixels (dots) arranged in such a way that they form a graphic image. Because of the very nature of bitmaps, the question of 'resolution' – the sharpness of an image expressed in dpi (dots per inch) – is very important. Bitmaps look best if they're displayed at their native resolution. Works 2000 can manipulate a wide variety of third-party bitmap graphics formats. These include: PCX, TIF and GIF.

Vector images

You can also insert vector graphics files into Word Processor documents. Vector images consist of and are defined by algebraic equations. They're less complex than bitmaps: they contain less detail. Vector files can also include bitmap information.

Irrespective of the format type, Works can incorporate images with the help of special 'filters'. These are special mini-programs whose job it is to translate third-party formats into a form which Works can use.

Brief notes on image formats

Works 2000 will happily import a wide selection of bitmap and vector graphic formats. These are some of the main formats:

Bitmap formats

PCX
: An old standby. Originated with PC Paintbrush, a paint program. Used for years to transfer graphics data between Windows applications. Supports compression.

TIFF
: Tagged Image File Format. Suffix: .TIF. If anything, even more widely used than PCX, across a whole range of platforms and applications. Supports numerous types and levels of compression.

Another format which the Word Processor can translate is Portable Network Graphics (.PNG).

This format supports high compression, making it very handy for use on the Web, but unfortunately is not supported by all browsers.

BMP
: Not as common as PCX and TIFF, but still popular. One drawback: sometimes, compression isn't normally available.

GIF
: Graphics Interchange Format. Developed for the online transmission of graphics data across the CompuServe network. Just about any Windows program – and a lot more besides – will read GIF. Disadvantage: it can't handle more than 256 colours. One of the few graphics formats which can be used in HTML (HyperText Markup Language) documents on the World Wide Web. Compression is supported.

The main supported vector format is Windows Metafile (suffix .WMF).

This format is used for information exchange between just about all Windows programs, and often produces files which are much smaller than the equivalent bitmaps (though not because of compression – there isn't any).

PCD
: (Kodak) PhotoCD. Used primarily to store photographs on CD.

JPEG
: Joint Photographic Experts Group. Suffix: .JPG. Used on the PC and Mac for the storage and display of photographs. One of the few graphics formats which can be used in HTML (HyperText Markup Language) documents on the World Wide Web. A very high level of compression is built into the format.

Inserting images – an overview

Works 2000 lets you insert the following into your Word Processor documents:

- clip art

- pictures

You insert pictures via a separate dialog – see pages 68-69.

By clip art, Works means the image files supplied on the program CD, some of which will have been automatically copied to your hard disk during installation.

The term 'pictures', on the other hand, refers to third-party graphics formats (e.g. TIFF and PCX).

You add clip art with the use of the Clip Gallery. The Clip Gallery:

— provides a visual catalogue of clip art on your system

— lets you view images as 'thumbnails' (small icons representing clip art)

— makes it easy to keep track of clip art

The Clip Gallery displaying clip art images:

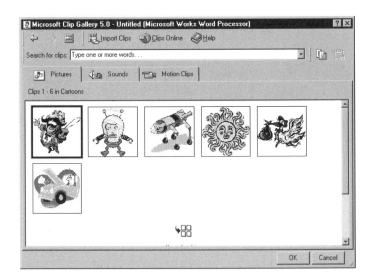

In the Clip Gallery, clip art images are organised under a large number of categories. Examples are:

- Animals

- Backgrounds

- Borders & Frames

- Cartoons

- Food & Dining

- Gestures

- Home & Family

- Industry

- Metaphors

- Music

- Nature

- People at Work

- Science & Technology

- Weather

If you don't have the Works 2000 CD in your CD-ROM drive, far fewer images (around 100) are available.

Because Works 2000 supplies so many clip art images, it's important to be able to carry out image housekeeping.

You can:

— allocate a different category to a given clip art image

— create new categories

— rename categories

— remove categories

Inserting clip art

Make sure the Works 2000 CD is in the relevant drive. Within the relevant Word Processor document, do the following:

Click where you want the clip art inserted

Pull down the Insert menu and do the following:

2 Click here

3 Click here

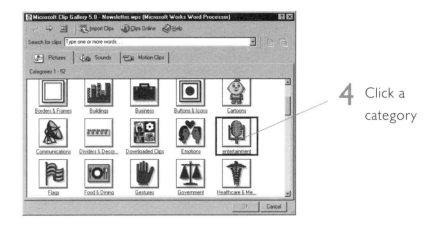

4 Click a category

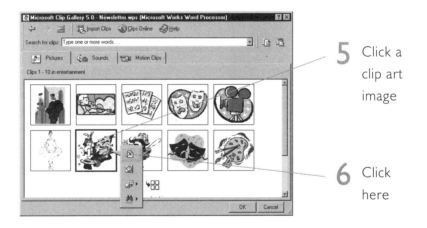

5 Click a clip art image

6 Click here

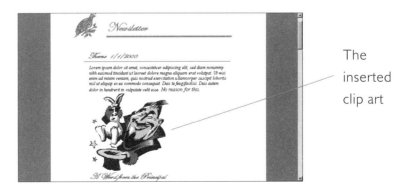

The inserted clip art

Inserting pictures

Make sure the Works 2000 CD is in its drive. Within the relevant Word Processor document, do the following:

Click where you want the picture inserted

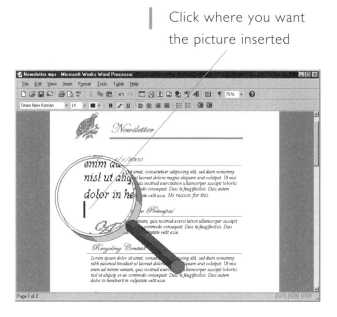

Pull down the Insert menu and do the following:

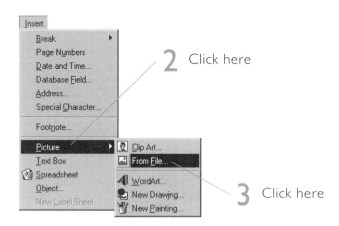

2 Click here

3 Click here

4 Click here. In the drop-down list, click the drive which hosts the picture

Re step 5 – you may have to double-click one or more folders first, to locate the picture you want to open.

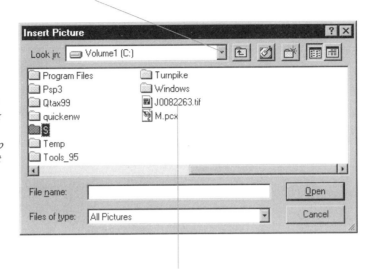

5 Double-click a picture

The inserted picture:

Gallery housekeeping

You can carry out housekeeping operations on categories.

Applying new categories to images

Launch the Clip Gallery in the usual way. Then do the following:

You can also download clips from the Web. First ensure your Internet connection is live. Click this button:

in the Gallery. If this message appears:

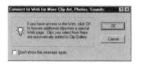

click OK. Your browser now launches. Follow the on-screen instructions.

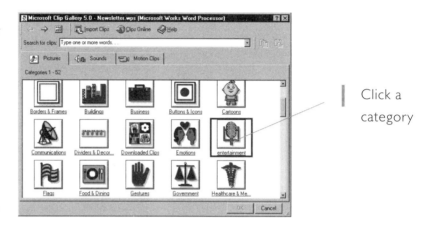

1 Click a category

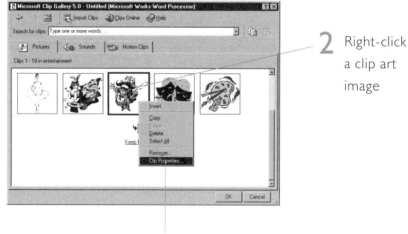

2 Right-click a clip art image

To close the Clip Gallery, click the following button in the top right-hand corner:

3 Select Clip Properties

...cont'd

Re step 5 – you can also deselect existing category

allocations.

4 Select the
   Categories tab

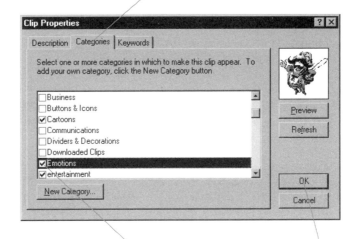

5 Select one or more
   new categories

6 Click here

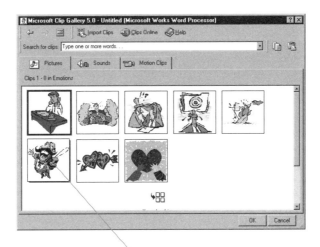

Here, the clip art selected in
step 2 has been added to
the Emotions category

Creating new image categories

Launch the Clip Gallery in the usual way. Then do the following:

The New Category icon is only available in the Clip Gallery's Home page.
If the Home page isn't currently on-screen, press Alt+Home.

1 Click the New Category icon

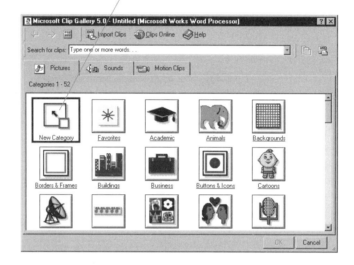

2 Name the new category

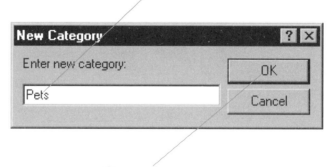

3 Click here

Renaming image categories

Launch the Clip Gallery in the usual way. Then do the following:

1 Select a category

To delete a category (but not the clips it contains), follow step 1. In step 2, select Delete Category. In the message which launches, click OK.

2 Click Rename Category

3 Rename the category

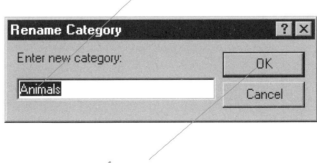

4 Click here

Using keywords

Clips in the Clip Gallery can (and do) have keywords associated with them (this means that, if you want to find a specific picture, you can run a keyword search – see the facing page). You can add additional keywords to any clip art image.

Adding keywords to clip art

Do the following:

1 If the Clip Gallery isn't currently open, pull down the Insert menu and click Picture, Clip Art

2 Follow steps 1-3 on page 70

3 Activate the Keywords tab

*To delete a keyword, highlight it here:
Now click:*

Remove Keyword

The keyword is removed immediately.

Repeat steps 4-6 for as many keywords as you want to add.

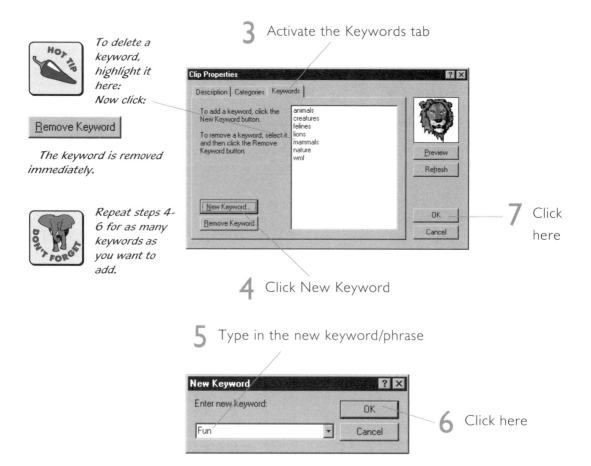

7 Click here

4 Click New Keyword

5 Type in the new keyword/phrase

6 Click here

Searching for keywords

To search for clip art by one or more keywords, do the following:

1 If the Clip Gallery isn't currently open, pull down the Insert menu and click Picture, Clip Art

2 Type in one or more keywords (or a key phrase), then press Enter

Moving the mouse pointer over a clip produces a box listing the first few associated keywords:

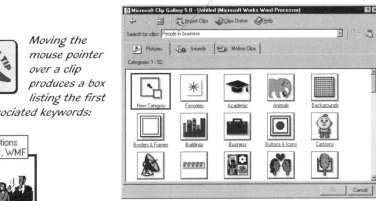

The end result:

If you want to see additional Gallery clips, click this button:

Keep Looking

after the final clip.

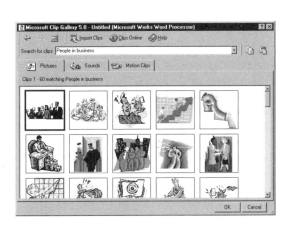

The Gallery displays all clips associated with the keyword(s)

Importing clip art into the Gallery

To add new images to the Gallery, do the following:

I   If the Clip Gallery isn't currently open, pull down the Insert menu and click Picture, Clip Art

3   Click Import Clips

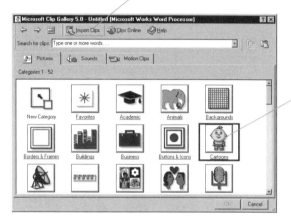

Re step 5 –
you may have
to double-click
one or more
folders first, to
locate the clip(s) you want
to import.

2   Click the category into which you want the clip inserted

Re step 5 –
you can import
more than 1
clip at a time.
Hold down Ctrl
as you select them.

4   Click here; select a drive

After step 7,
the Clip
Properties
dialog launches.
Do the
following, as appropriate:

• *activate the Description tab and type in brief details of the clip*

• *activate the Categories tab and select one or more extra categories, and/or;*

• *activate the Keywords tab and follows steps 4-6 on page 74 as often as necessary*

Finally, click OK.

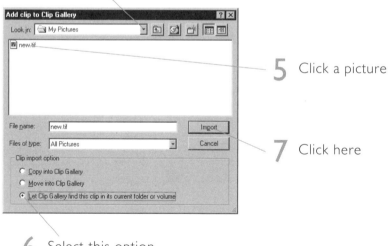

5   Click a picture

7   Click here

6   Select this option

Manipulating images – an overview

Once you've inserted images into a document, you can work with them in a variety of ways. You can:

- rescale them

- specify how text flows around them

- apply a border

- move them

Selecting an image

To carry out any of these operations, you have to select the relevant image first. To do this, simply position the mouse pointer over the image and left-click once. Works surrounds the image with eight handles. These are positioned at the four corners, and midway on each side:

Handles

Handles

Rescaling images

There are two ways in which you can rescale images:

- proportionally, where the height/width ratio remains constant

- disproportionately, where the height/width ratio is disrupted (this is sometimes called 'warping' or 'skewing')

To rescale a image, first select it. Then move the mouse pointer over:

You can also use a special dialog to rescale images — see the facing page.

— one of the corner handles, if you want to rescale the image proportionally

or

— one of the handles in the middle of the sides, if you want to warp it

In either eventuality, the mouse pointer changes to a double-headed arrow. Click and hold down the left mouse button. Drag outwards to increase the image size or inwards to decrease it.

Release the mouse button to confirm the change.

Here, the image from page 77 has been skewed from the right inwards

Rescaling images – the dialog route

You can use a special dialog to rescale images, a method which allows much greater precision.

First, select the image you want to amend. Pull down the Format menu and to the following:

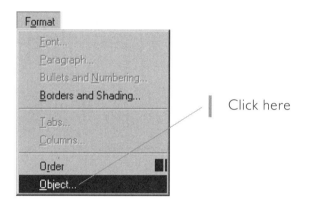

Click here

2 Ensure the Size tab is active

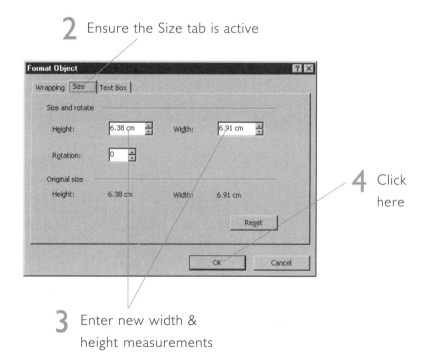

4 Click here

3 Enter new width & height measurements

Bordering images

By default, the Word Processor does not apply a border to inserted pictures. However, you can apply a wide selection of graphical borders with decorative shapes and lines – Works 2000 calls these Border Art.

When you've applied a Border Art, you can specify the width (as points, like type).

Applying a border

First, select the picture you want to border. Then pull down the Format menu and click Borders and Shading. Now do the following:

You can only border pictures or clip art with the procedures described here if you've applied Square or Tight text wrap to them – see pages 82-83.

If, however, a picture has had the 'In line with text' text wrap applied, Works regards it as being part of the paragraph it occupies. For this reason:

- *the available border options are those of text paragraphs – follow steps 1-5 on page 46 instead, and;*

- *the whole paragraph (not just the graphic) is bordered*

1 Click here; in the list, select a Border Art style

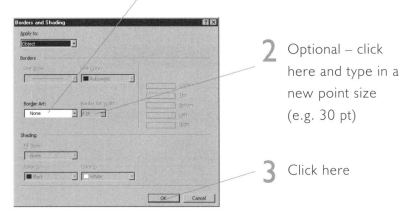

2 Optional – click here and type in a new point size (e.g. 30 pt)

3 Click here

A clip art image after a Border Art has been applied

Moving images

You can easily move images from one location on the page to another.

First, click the image to select it. Move the mouse pointer over it; it changes to a pointing arrow. Left-click once and hold down the button. Drag the image to its new location.

Magnified view
of Move cursor

Release the mouse button to confirm the move.

Problems with Move operations?

If you find that dragging has no effect, this is probably because the 'In line with text' text wrap option is in force (in other words, Works 2000 is treating the graphic as part of the host paragraph). Do the following to correct this situation:

1 Select the graphic

2 Apply Square or Tight text wrap to it – for how to do this, see page 83.

3 Repeat the Move operation

Wrapping text around images

If you insert clip art or pictures into documents which contain text, it's often useful to have the text flow ('wrap') around the graphics rather than through them. There are three text wrap options:

In line with text (no text to the side)

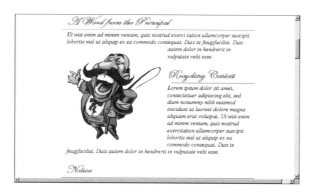

Square (the image is bounded by an imaginary box and the text wraps round this)

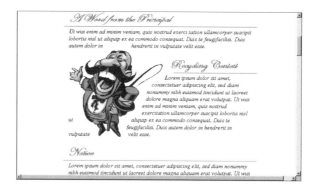

Tight (the text contours around the image's shape)

Applying text wrap

First, select an image. Pull down the Format menu and do the following:

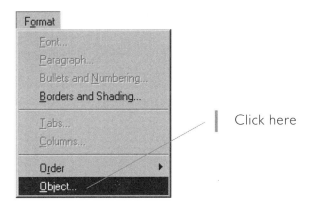

Click here

2 Ensure the Wrapping tab is active

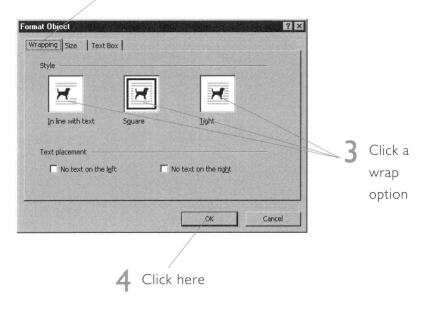

Re step 3 – if you select Square or Tight, you can disable text wrap for the left or right side of the image.

Simply select one of the following:

• No text on the left, or;

• No text on the right

3 Click a wrap option

4 Click here

Page setup – an overview

You can control the following aspects of page layout in the Word Processor module:

- the top, bottom, left and/or right page margins

- the distance between the top page edge and the top edge of the header

- the distance between the bottom page edge and bottom edge of the footer

The illustration below shows these page components:

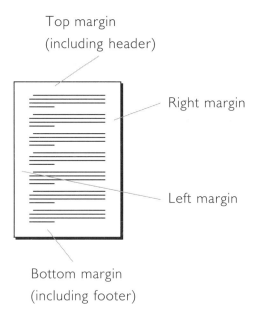

Top margin
(including header)

Right margin

Left margin

Bottom margin
(including footer)

You can also specify:

— the overall page size (inclusive of margins and headers/footers)

— the page orientation ('landscape' or 'portrait')

If none of the supplied page sizes is suitable, you can even customise your own.

Specifying margins

Margin settings are the framework on which indents and tabs are based.

All documents have margins, because printing on the whole of a sheet is both unsightly and – in the case of many printers, since the mechanism has to grip the page – impossible. Documents need a certain amount of 'white space' (the unprinted portion of the page) to balance the areas which contain text and graphics. Without this, they can't be visually effective.

As a result, it's important to set margins correctly. Fortunately, the Word Processor module makes the job of changing margin settings easy. Note, however, that you can only adjust margin settings on a document-wide basis (i.e. not for individual pages).

Customising margins

Pull down the File menu and click Page Setup. Now carry out steps 1-3 below:

1 Ensure the Margins tab is active

2 Enter new margin settings

Optionally, type in header or footer margin settings here:

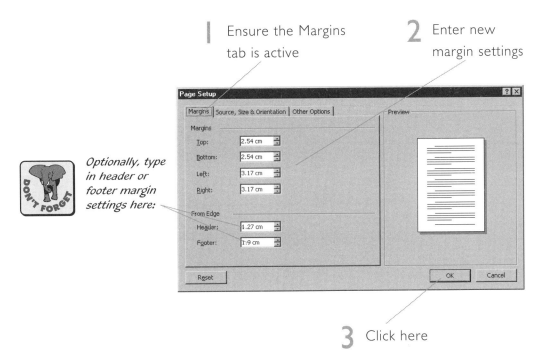

3 Click here

Specifying the page size

The Word Processor comes with 17 preset page sizes. These are suitable for most purposes. However, if you need to you can also set up your own page definition.

There are two aspects to every page size:

- a vertical measurement

- a horizontal measurement

There are two possible orientations:

Portrait orientation

Landscape orientation

Setting the page size

Pull down the File menu and do the following:

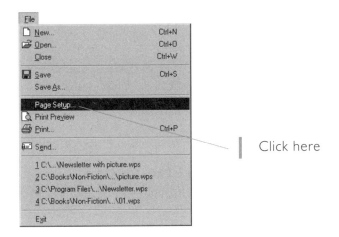

| Click here

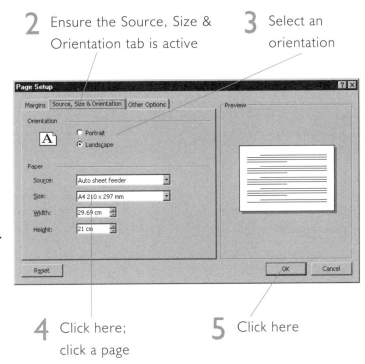

2 Ensure the Source, Size & Orientation tab is active

3 Select an orientation

To create your own page size, click Custom in step 4. Then type in the appropriate measurements in the Width & Height fields. Finally, carry out step 5.

4 Click here; click a page size in the list

5 Click here

Using Print Preview

Although you can't specify the precise number of pages displayed, you can specify:

- *One Page – only one page is shown*
- *Two Pages (only in step 1 on the facing page) – two pages are shown, or;*
- *Multiple Pages – the Word Processor displays as many full pages as possible*

The Word Processor provides a special view mode called Print Preview. This displays the active document exactly as it will look when printed.

Use Print Preview as a final check just before you print your document.

When you're using Print Preview, you can zoom in or out on the active page. What you can't do, however, is:

- specify the number of pages displayed

- edit or revise the active document

Launching Print Preview

Pull down the File menu and click Print Preview. This is the result:

If the Print Preview command is greyed out and therefore unavailable, check that:

- *your printer is connected properly, and;*
- *the relevant printer driver (the software that runs the printer) is installed and operative*

Click Close to leave Print Preview

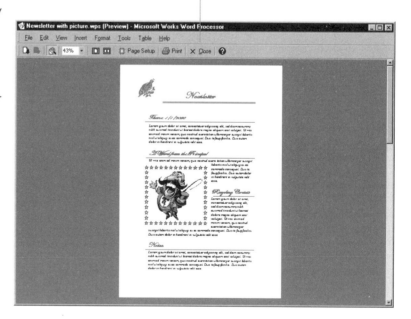

You can use a keyboard shortcut to leave Print Preview mode. Simply press Esc.

Zooming in or out in Print Preview

There are two methods you can use here.

Using the mouse
Do the following:

If step 2 does not work, click the following button on the dedicated toolbar:

Now repeat step 2.

Move the mouse pointer over the page (it changes to a magnifying glass)

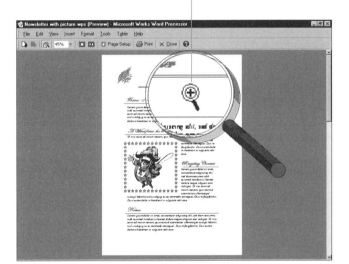

Repeating step 2 returns the magnification to the original level.

2 Left-click once to increase the magnification

Using the Print Preview toolbar
Launch Print Preview. Then carry out the following actions:

Re step 1 on the right – you can also select a pre-defined Zoom level (e.g. 200% or Page Width) instead.
  (See also the DON'T FORGET tip on the facing page.)

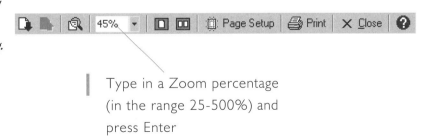

Type in a Zoom percentage (in the range 25-500%) and press Enter

Changing pages in Print Preview

In Print Preview, you can also step backwards and forwards through the active document as often as necessary.

There are three methods you can use (in descending order of usefulness).

Using the dedicated toolbar
Carry out the following actions:

Depending on your location within the document (and the number of pages), one of these buttons may be greyed out, and therefore unavailable.

Click here to jump to the next page

Click here to jump to the previous page

Using the keyboard

In a magnified page view, the Page Up and Page Down keys move through the current page instead.

You can use the following keyboard shortcuts:

Page Up   Moves to the previous page (unavailable within a magnified page view)

Page Down   Moves to the next page (unavailable within a magnified page view)

Using the scrollbars
When you're working with a magnified view of a page, use the vertical and/or horizontal scrollbars (using standard Windows techniques) to move up or down within the page.

Printer setup

Most Word Processor documents need to be printed eventually. Before you can begin printing, however, you must ensure that:

The question of which printer you select affects how the document displays in Print Preview mode.

- the correct printer is selected (if you have more than one installed)

- the correct printer settings are in force

Works 2000 calls these collectively the 'printer setup'.

Irrespective of the printer selected, the settings vary in accordance with the job in hand. For example, most printer drivers (the software which 'drives' the printer) allow you to specify whether or not you want pictures printed. Additionally, they often allow you to specify the resolution or print quality of the output.

Selecting the printer and/or settings

Just before you're ready to print a document, pull down the File menu and click Print. Now do the following:

Re step 2 – for how to adjust printer settings, see your printer's manual.

1 Click here; select the printer you want from the list

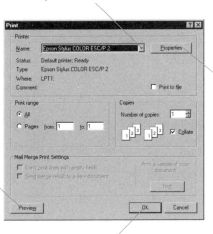

You can launch Print Preview from within the Print dialog. Simply click here before step 3:

2 Click here to adjust the printer settings (then complete the dialog which launches)

Set any print options which are required before carrying out step 3 (see 'Customised Printing' on page 93 for how to do this).

3 Click here to begin printing

Printing – an overview

Once the active document is how you want it (and you've customised the printer setup appropriately), the next stage is to print it out. The Word Processor makes this process easy and straightforward. It lets you set a variety of options before you do so – refer to the facing page for how to do this.

Alternatively, you can simply opt to print your document with the default options in force (the Word Processor provides a 'fast track' approach) – see page 94 for how to do this.

Available print options include:

- the number of copies you want printed

- whether you want the copies 'collated'. This is the process whereby Works 2000 prints one full copy at a time. For instance, if you're printing three copies of a 40-page document, Works prints pages 1-40 of the first document, followed by pages 1-40 of the second and pages 1-40 of the third...

  (Collation is only available in those documents which have more than one page.)

- which pages you want printed. You can specify unbroken page ranges (e.g. 3-23) but not sporadic ones (e.g. 3, 6 and 8-12)

- printing to a file instead of directly to a printer. When you exercise this option, a special dialog launches in which you specify a file name for the Word Processor to use. All print files have the extension: .PRN

You can 'mix and match' these, as appropriate.

Customised printing

If you need to set revised print options before printing, pull down the File menu and click Print. Now carry out steps 1-3 below, as appropriate. To inspect your document in Print Preview mode before printing, follow steps 4-5. Finally (if you haven't performed steps 4-5) carry out step 6 to begin printing.

To print to a file instead of a printer, customise your print job in the usual way. Then select Print to file and carry out step 6. The Print to file dialog appears. Select a drive/ folder combination for the new file, then name it. Click OK. The Word Processor now saves your print job as a file.

3 Type in start and end pages

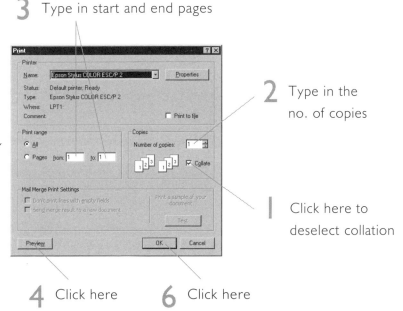

2 Type in the no. of copies

1 Click here to deselect collation

4 Click here

6 Click here

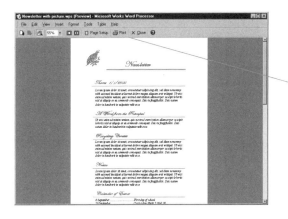

5 Click Close to close Preview without printing or Print to print the document immediately

Printing – the fast track approach

Since documents and printing needs vary dramatically, it's often necessary to customise print options before you begin printing. For how to set your own print options, see page 93.

On the other hand, there are occasions when you'll merely want to print out your work (often for proofing purposes) bypassing the Print dialog and with the current settings applying. For this reason, Works 2000 provides a method which is quicker and easier to use.

Printing with the current print options

First, ensure your printer is ready, and your document is ready to print. Make sure the Standard toolbar is visible. (If it isn't, pull down the View menu and click Toolbar, Standard).

Now do the following:

Click here

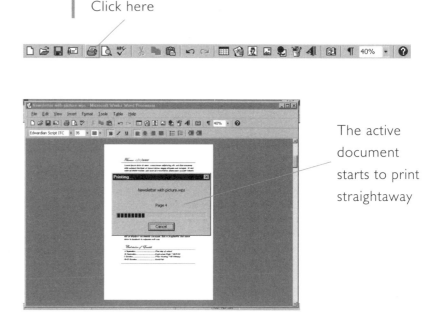

The active document starts to print straightaway

The Spreadsheet

This chapter gives you the basics of using the Spreadsheet module. You'll learn how to work with data and formulas, and how to move around in spreadsheets. You'll also discover how to locate data, and make it more visually effective by converting it to charts. Finally, you'll customise page layout/printing.

Covers

The Spreadsheet screen | 96

Entering and modifying data | 97

Working with cell ranges | 100

Moving around in spreadsheets | 101

Changing Zoom levels | 103

Selection techniques | 105

Formulas and functions | 107

Cell protection | 111

Working with rows and columns | 113

Fills and AutoFill | 115

Headers and footers | 117

Formatting | 119

Find and search-and-replace operations | 126

Charting | 128

Page setup and printing | 133

Chapter Three

The Spreadsheet screen

Below is a detailed illustration of the Spreadsheet screen.

Title bar   Menu bar   Column headings

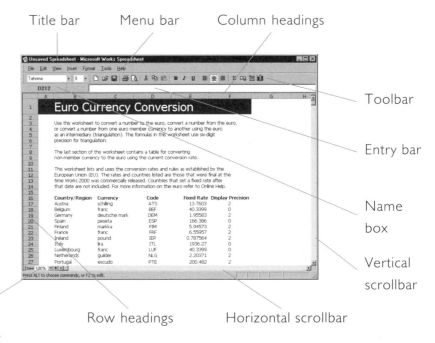

Toolbar

Entry bar

Name box

Vertical scrollbar

Row headings   Horizontal scrollbar

This is the Zoom Area: The screen components here are used to adjust magnification levels. See pages 103-104.

Some of these – e.g. the scrollbars – are standard to just about all programs which run under Windows. One – the Toolbar – can be hidden, if required.

Specifying whether the Toolbar displays

Pull down the View menu. Then do the following:

The tick signifies that the Toolbar is currently visible.

Click here to view or hide the Toolbar

Entering data

Columns are vertical, rows horizontal. Each spreadsheet can have as many as 256 columns and 16,384 rows, making a grand total of 4,194,304 cells.

You can insert the Euro symbol into spreadsheets. Fonts which support this include:

- *Arial*
- *Courier New*
- *Impact*
- *Tahoma, and;*
- *Times New Roman*

To insert the Euro symbol, press the Num Lock key on your keyboard. Hold down Alt and press 0128 (consecutively). Release Alt and turn off Num Lock.

An inserted Euro symbol

When you start the Works 2000 Spreadsheet module, you can use the Task Launcher to create a new blank spreadsheet (see Chapter 1 for how to do this). The result will look like this:

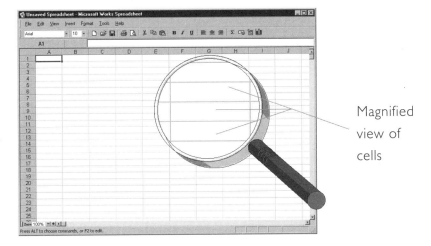

Magnified view of cells

This means that you can start entering data immediately.

In the Spreadsheet module, you can enter the following basic data types:

- values (i.e. numbers)

- text (e.g. headings and explanatory material)

- functions (e.g. Sine or Cosine)

- formulas (combinations of values, text and functions)

You enter data into 'cells'. Cells are formed where rows and columns intersect. In the most basic sense, collections of rows/columns and cells are known as spreadsheets.

Although you can enter data *directly* into a cell (by clicking in it, typing it in and pressing Enter), there's another method you can use which is often easier. The Spreadsheet provides a special screen component known as the Entry bar.

The illustration below shows the end of a blank spreadsheet. Some sample text has been inserted into cell IV16384 (note that the Name box tells you which cell is currently active):

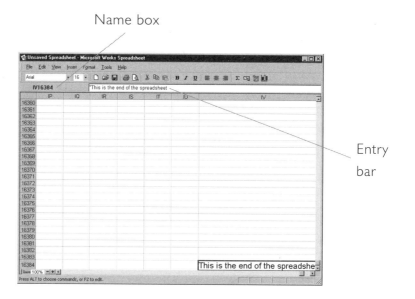

Name box

Entry bar

Entering data via the Entry bar

You can use a keyboard route to confirm operations in the Entry bar. Simply press Return. (Press Esc to cancel them.)

Click the cell you want to insert data into. Click the Entry bar. Type in the data. Then follow step 1 below. If you decide to cancel the operation, follow step 2 instead:

Click here

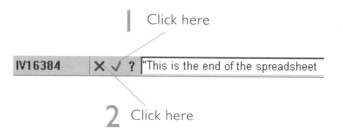

2 Click here

Modifying existing data

You can spell-check spreadsheet contents. Press F7. Complete the Spelling dialog in line with steps 1-4 on page 59 (the dialog is rather different, but the procedures are basically the same).

To launch the Financial Worksheets Wizard, click Programs in the Task Launcher. Select Works Spreadsheet, Financial worksheets. Now click the Start button and follow the on-screen instructions.

You can 'freeze' row/column titles so that they remain on screen when you move to other parts of the active spreadsheet.

Select the row below the row you want to freeze, or the column to the right of the column you want to freeze. Pull down the Format menu and click Freeze Titles.

To unfreeze all frozen titles, pull down the Format menu and deselect Freeze Titles.

You can amend the contents of a cell in two ways:

* via the Entry bar

* from within the cell

When you use either of these methods, the Spreadsheet enters a special state known as Edit Mode.

Amending existing data using the Entry bar

Click the cell whose contents you want to change. Then click in the Entry bar. Make the appropriate revisions and/or additions. Then press Return. The relevant cell is updated.

Amending existing data internally

Click the cell whose contents you want to change. Press F2. Make the appropriate revisions and/or additions *within the cell*. Then press Return.

The illustration below shows a section of a spreadsheet created with the Financial Worksheets Wizard.

A magnified view of cell D15 in Edit Mode

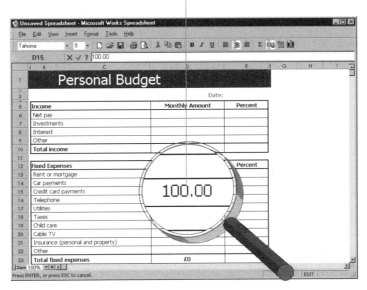

Working with cell ranges

By default, to make the underlying structure of a spreadsheet's component cells more visible Works 2000 displays gridlines on-screen:

When you're working with more than one cell, it's often convenient and useful to organise them in 'ranges'.

A range is a rectangular arrangement of cells. In the illustration below, cells B11, C11, D11, E11, F11, G11, B12, C12, D12, E12, F12 and G12 have been selected.

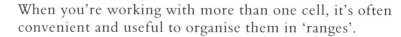

A selected cell range

Gridlines

To hide gridlines (or to make them visible again), pull down the View menu and click Gridlines.

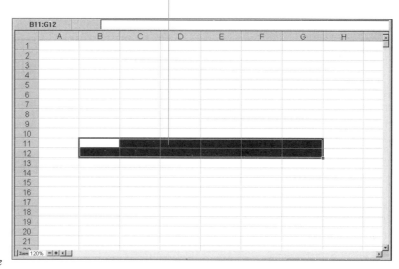

Cells in a selected range are coloured black, with the exception of the first.

Cell 'shorthand'

The above description of the relevant cells is very cumbersome. It's much more useful to use a form of shorthand. The Spreadsheet module (using the start and end cells as reference points) refers to these cells as: B11:G12

This notation system makes it much easier to refer to sizeable cell ranges.

You can name ranges, for even greater ease of use. To do this, select the range. Pull down the Insert menu and click Range Name. In the Name field in the Range Name dialog, type in a name. Click OK.

Moving around in spreadsheets

Spreadsheets can be huge. Moving to cells which happen currently to be visible is easy: you simply click in the relevant cell. However, the Spreadsheet module provides several techniques you can use to jump to less accessible areas.

Using the scrollbars
Use any of the following methods:

1. To scroll quickly to another section of the active spreadsheet, drag the scroll box along the scrollbar until you reach it

2. To move one window to the left or right, click to the left or right of the scroll box in the horizontal scrollbar

3. To move one window up or down, click above or below the scroll box in the vertical scrollbar

4. To move up or down by one row, click the arrows in the vertical scrollbar

5. To move left or right by one column, click the arrows in the horizontal scrollbar

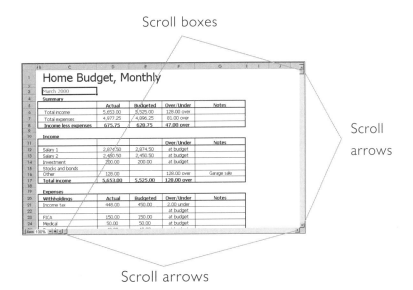

Scroll boxes

Scroll arrows

Scroll arrows

Using the keyboard

You can use the following techniques:

1. Use the cursor keys to move one cell left, right, up or down

2. Hold down Ctrl as you use 1. above; this jumps to the edge of the current section (e.g. if cell B11 is active and you hold down Ctrl as you press ➔, Works 2000 jumps to IV11, the last cell in row 11)

3. Press Home to jump to the first cell in the active row, or Ctrl+Home to move to A1

4. Press Page Up or Page Down to move up or down by one screen

5. Press Ctrl+Page Down to move one screen to the right, or Ctrl+Page Up to move one screen to the left

You can use a keyboard shortcut to launch the Go To dialog. Simply press F5, or Ctrl+G.

Using the Go To dialog

The Spreadsheet provides a special dialog which you can use to specify precise cell destinations.

Pull down the Edit menu and click Go To. Now do the following:

Re step 1 – a cell's 'reference' (or 'address') identifies it in relation to its position in a spreadsheet, e.g. B11 or H23.

You can also type in cell ranges here (e.g. B11:C15), or range names.

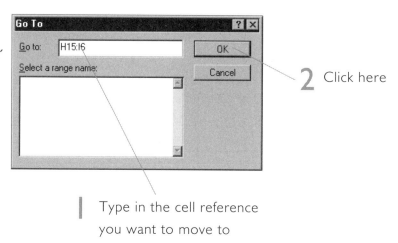

2 Click here

Type in the cell reference you want to move to

Changing Zoom levels

The ability to vary the level of magnification for the active document is especially useful for spreadsheets, which very often occupy more space than can be accommodated on-screen at any given time. Sometimes, it's helpful to 'zoom out' (i.e. decrease the magnification) so that you can take an overview; at other times, you'll need to 'zoom in' (increase the magnification) to work in greater detail.

You can alter magnification levels in the Spreadsheet module:

- with the use of the Zoom Area

- with the Zoom dialog

For more information on how to find the Zoom Area, see the illustration on page 96.

Using the Zoom Area

You can use the Zoom Area (at the base of the screen) to alter zoom levels with the minimum of effort. Carry out step 1 OR 2, or steps 3 AND 4, as appropriate:

Re step 4 – clicking Custom produces the Zoom dialog. (See overleaf for how to use this.)

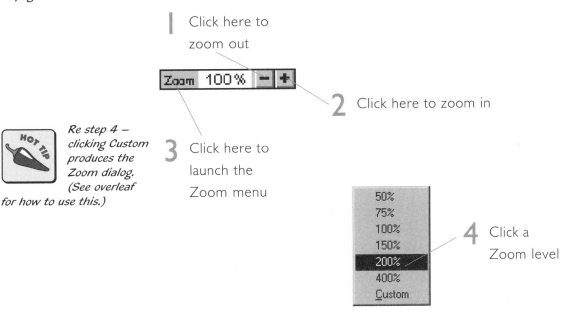

1 Click here to zoom out

2 Click here to zoom in

3 Click here to launch the Zoom menu

4 Click a Zoom level

50%
75%
100%
150%
200%
400%
Custom

Using the Zoom dialog

Using the Zoom dialog, you can perform the following Zoom actions. You can:

Zoom settings have no effect on the way spreadsheets print.

- choose from preset Zoom levels (e.g. 200%, 100%, 75%)

- specify your own Zoom percentage

If you want to impose your own, custom zoom level, it's probably easier, quicker and more convenient to use the Zoom dialog.

Pull down the View menu and click Zoom. Now carry out step 1 or 2 below. Finally, follow step 3:

3 Click here

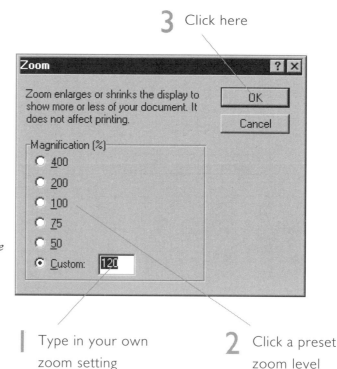

Re step 1 – entries must lie in the range 25%-1000%

| Type in your own zoom setting

2 Click a preset zoom level

Selection techniques

Before you can carry out any editing operations on cells in the Spreadsheet module, you have to select them first. Selecting a single cell is very easy: you merely click in it. However, there are a variety of selection techniques which you can use to select more than one cell simultaneously.

Selecting cell ranges with the mouse

The easiest way to select more than one cell at a time is to use the mouse.

Click in the first cell in the range; hold down the left mouse button and drag over the remaining cells. Release the mouse button.

Selecting cell ranges with the keyboard

There are two separate techniques you can use:

With the exception of the first cell, a selected range is filled with black.

- Position the cell pointer over the first cell in the range. Hold down one Shift key as you use the relevant cursor key to extend the selection. Release the keys when the correct selection has been defined

- Position the cell pointer over the first cell in the range. Press F8 to enter Selection mode. Use the cursor keys to define the selection area (see the illustration below). Finally, press F8 again to leave Selection mode

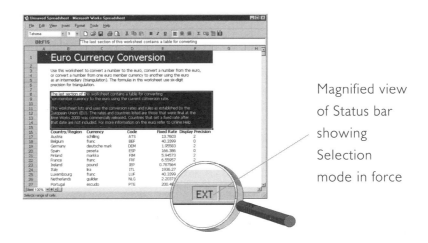

Magnified view of Status bar showing Selection mode in force

Selecting a single row or column

To select every cell within a row or column automatically, click the row or column heading.

Column heading

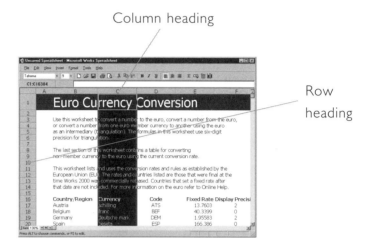

Row heading

Selecting multiple rows or columns

To select more than one row or column, click the row or column heading. Hold down the left mouse button and drag to select adjacent rows or columns.

Selecting an entire spreadsheet

Click the Select All button:

You can use a keyboard shortcut to select every cell automatically.
Simply press Ctrl+A, or Ctrl+Shift+F8.

A magnified view of the Select All button

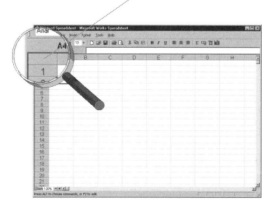

Formulas – an overview

Formulas are cell entries which define how other values relate to each other.

As a very simple example, consider the following:

Cell G16 has been defined so that it multiplies the contents of cells D16 and H16. Obviously, in this instance you could insert the result easily enough yourself because the values are so small, and because we're only dealing with a small number of cells. But what happens if the cell values are larger and/or more numerous, or – more to the point – if they're liable to change frequently?

The answer is to insert a formula which carries out the necessary calculation automatically.

The 'H16*D16' component tells Works 2000 to multiply the contents of the two cells. The 'IF' before the bracket is the conditional operator.

If you look at the Entry bar in the illustration, you'll see the formula which does this:

=IF(H16,H16*D16,"")

This is a fairly complex formula. Basically, it instructs Works 2000 to inspect cell H16. If an entry is found, the contents should be multiplied by the contents of D16, and the results displayed.

Inserting a formula

Arguments (e.g. cell references) relating to functions are always contained in brackets.

All formulas in the Spreadsheet begin with an equals sign. This is usually followed by a permutation of the following:

- an operand (cell reference, e.g. B4)

- a function (e.g. the summation function, SUM)

- an arithmetical operator ($+$, $-$, $/$, $*$ and $^$)

- comparison operators ($=$, $<$, $>$, $<=$, $>=$ and $<>$)

The Spreadsheet supports a very wide range of functions organised into numerous categories. For more information on how to insert functions, see the facing page.

The mathematical operators are (in the order in which they appear in the bulleted list): *plus, minus, divide, multiply* and *exponential.*

The comparison operators are (in the order in which they appear in the list): *equals, less than, greater than, less than or equal to, greater than or equal to* and *not equal to.*

There are two ways to enter formulas:

Entering a formula directly into the cell

Click the cell in which you want to insert a formula. Then type $=$, followed by your formula. When you've finished, press Return.

Entering a formula into the Entry bar

Using the Entry bar method is usually the most convenient.

Click the cell in which you want to insert a formula. Then click in the Entry bar. Type $=$, followed by your formula. When you've finished, press Return or do the following in the Entry bar:

Click here

Functions – an overview

Functions are pre-defined, built-in tools which accomplish specific tasks and then display the result. These tasks are very often calculations; occasionally, however, they're considerably more generalised (e.g. some functions simply return dates and/or times). In effect, functions replace one or more formulas.

The Spreadsheet module organises its functions under the following headings:

- Financial

- Date and Time

- Math and Trig

- Statistical

- Lookup and Ref

- Text

- Logical

- Informational

You can, however, have Works 2000 display formulas/functions in situ within the spreadsheet. Simply pull down the View menu and click Formulas.

Formulas showing in cells

(To re-hide formulas, repeat the above.)

Works 2000 provides a special shortcut (called Easy Calc) which makes entering functions much easier and more straightforward. Easy Calc is very useful for the following reasons:

— It provides access to a large number of functions from a centralised source

— It ensures that functions are entered with the correct syntax

Functions can only be used in formulas. Note, however, that the result displays in the host cell, rather than the underlying function/formula.

Using Easy Calc

Inserting a function with Easy Calc

At the relevant juncture during the process of inserting a formula, pull down the Tools menu and click Easy Calc. Now carry out step 1 OR 2 below:

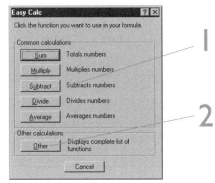

If you follow step 2, Works 2000 launches the Insert Function dialog. Pick a function category in the Category field, then select the relevant function in the Choose a function box. Click Insert.
Now follow steps 3-6.

1 Click the appropriate function type

2 Click Other if you need an unusual function

Now complete the following dialogs (the contents vary with the function selected):

Re step 3 – click the cells (within the spreadsheet itself) which host the values you want to include in the function, or define the appropriate cell range.
Works 2000 inserts the cell references and the relevant operator(s) into the dialog.

Re step 5 – alternatively, click the cell within the spreadsheet itself.

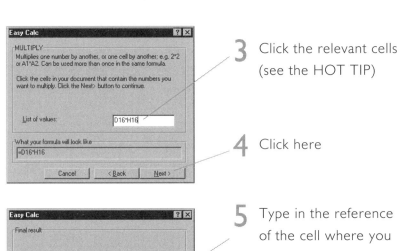

3 Click the relevant cells (see the HOT TIP)

4 Click here

5 Type in the reference of the cell where you want the function inserted

6 Click here to insert the function

Cell protection

Specific cells can be protected so that their contents are not overwritten. This is a two-stage process:

By default, all spreadsheet cells are locked, but not protected.

1. 'unlocking' those cells which you'll want to amend later (and therefore don't want to protect)

2. protecting the cells which are still locked (cell locking is ineffective until you do this)

You can also protect the active spreadsheet in its entirety.

Unlocking and protecting specific cells

Select the cells you *don't* want to protect. Pull down the Format menu and carry out steps 1, 2 and 4 below. Now (ensuring no cells are selected) pull down the Format menu again and carry out steps 1, 3 and 4 below:

| Click here

2 Ensure Locked is deselected

Re step 3 – Works 2000 protects those cells which have not been unlocked in the first stage in this operation.

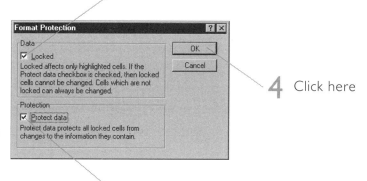

4 Click here

3 Ensure Protect Data is ticked

...cont'd

The procedures here assume that no cells have been unlocked (see page 111).

Protecting *all* cells in a spreadsheet

Pull down the Format menu and click Protection. Do the following:

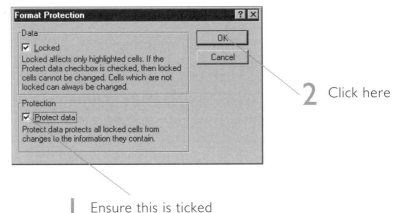

2 Click here

Ensure this is ticked

If you want to remove cell protection, follow steps 1-2 again. (In step 1, however, ensure Protect data isn't ticked).

The effects of cell protection

When you've protected cells, the following results apply:

1. any attempt to overwrite/edit a locked cell produces a special message:

Click here to return to the spreadsheet

2. when a locked cell is selected, certain menu commands are greyed out

Amending row/column sizes

Sooner or later, you'll find it necessary to change the dimensions of rows or columns. This necessity arises when there is too much data in cells to display adequately. You can enlarge or shrink single or multiple rows/columns.

Changing row height

To change one row's height, click the row heading. If you want to change multiple rows, hold down Shift and click the appropriate extra headings. Then pull down the Format menu and click Row Height. Carry out the following steps:

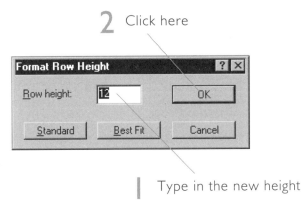

2 Click here

Type in the new height

Works 2000 has a useful 'best fit' feature. Simply click Best Fit in either dialog to have the row(s) or column(s) adjust themselves automatically to their contents.

Changing column width

To change one column's width, click the column heading. If you want to change multiple columns, hold down Shift and click the appropriate extra headings. Then pull down the Format menu and click Column Width. Now do the following:

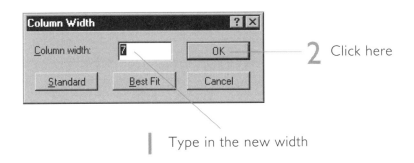

2 Click here

Type in the new width

Inserting rows or columns

You can insert additional rows or columns into spreadsheets.

Inserting a new row or column

First, select one or more cells within the row(s) or column(s) where you want to carry out the insert operation. Now pull down the Insert menu and carry out step 1 OR 2 below, as appropriate:

If you select cells in more than one row or column, Works 2000 inserts the equivalent number of new rows or columns.

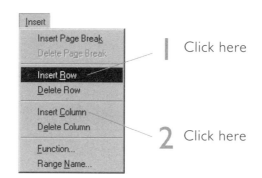

1 Click here

2 Click here

The new row(s) or column(s) are inserted immediately.

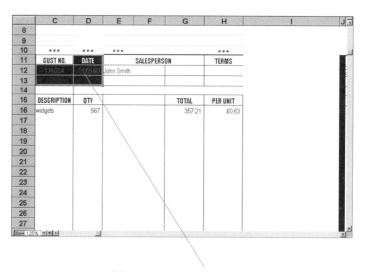

Here, two new columns or three new rows are being added

Working with fills

The Spreadsheet module lets you duplicate the contents of a selected cell down a column or across a row, easily and conveniently.

Use this technique to save time and effort.

Duplicating a cell

Click the cell whose contents you want to duplicate. Then move the mouse pointer over the appropriate border; the pointer changes to a cross and the word FILL appears:

Here, cell A3 has been selected.

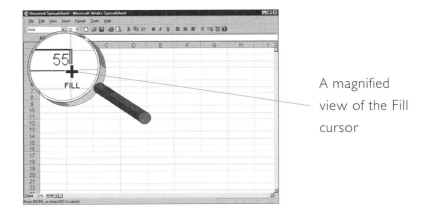

A magnified view of the Fill cursor

Click and hold down the button; drag the border over the cells into which you want the contents inserted. Release the button.

The contents of A3 have been copied to A4:A15.

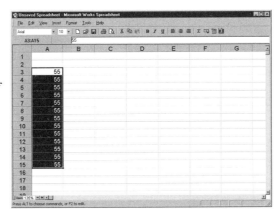

Using AutoFill

You can also carry out intelligent fills which *extrapolate* cell contents over the specified cells – Works calls these 'data series'. Look at the next illustration:

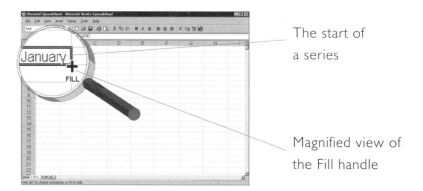

The start of a series

Magnified view of the Fill handle

If (as here) you wanted to insert month names progressively in successive cells in a column, you could do so manually. But there's a much easier way. You can use AutoFill.

Using AutoFill to create a series

In addition to months, data series can consist of the following:

- *numbers (e.g. 1, 2, 3, 4 etc.)*
- *days of the week*
- *years, and;*
- *alphanumeric combinations (e.g. Week 1, Week 2, Week 3 etc.)*

Type in the first element(s) of the series in a cell or consecutive cells. Select the cell(s). Then position the mouse pointer over the Fill handle in the bottom right-hand corner of the last cell (the pointer changes to a cross-hair). Hold down the left mouse button and drag the handle over the cells into which you want to extend the series. When you release the mouse button, Works 2000 extrapolates the initial entry or entries into the appropriate series.

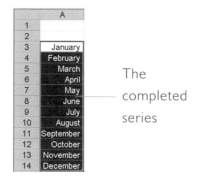

The completed series

Working with headers

To edit an existing header, simply follow the procedures outlined here; in step 1, amend the current header text as necessary.

You can have the Spreadsheet print text at the top of each page within a document; the area of the page where repeated text appears is called the 'header'. In the same way, you can have text printed at the base of each page; in this case, the relevant page area is called the 'footer'. Headers and footers are printed within the top and bottom page margins, respectively.

Inserting a header

Pull down the View menu and click Headers and Footers. Now do the following:

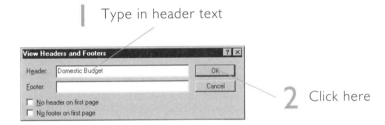

Type in header text

2 Click here

You can only view headers in Print Preview mode.

Viewing headers

Launch Print Preview mode – see page 138 for how to do this.

It isn't possible to amend the formatting of text in spreadsheet headers.

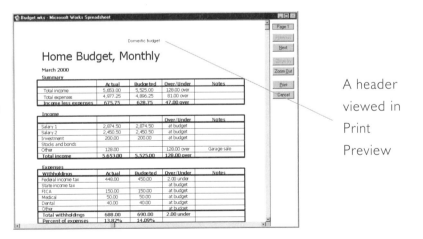

A header viewed in Print Preview

Working with footers

You can have the Spreadsheet automatically print text at the bottom of each page within a document; the area of the page where repeated text appears is called the 'footer'.

Footers are often used to display an abbreviated version of the spreadsheet's title.

Inserting a footer

Pull down the View menu and click Headers and Footers. Now do the following:

Type in footer text

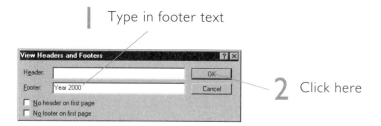

2 Click here

Viewing footers

Launch Print Preview mode – see page 138 for how to do this.

A footer viewed in Print Preview

Changing number formats

The Spreadsheet module lets you apply various formatting enhancements to cells and their contents. You can:

Number formats let you specify a variety of options. These include:

- specify a number format

- customise the font, type size and style of contents

- specify cell alignment

- border and/or shade cells

Fixed, Number, Percent, Currency & Exponential	*You specify the no. of decimal places*
Date & Time	*You specify the format (e.g. 17 April 2000 or 02:54 PM)*
Fraction	*You specify how fractions are rounded up*
True/False, General and Text	*No options*

Specifying a number format

You can customise the way cell contents (e.g. numbers and dates/times) display. For example, you can specify at what point numbers are rounded up. Available formats are organised under several general categories. These include: Date, Percent and Fraction.

Select the cells whose contents you want to customise. Pull down the Format menu and click Number. Now do the following:

1 Ensure the Number tab is active

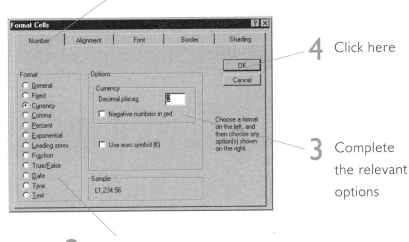

Re step 3 – the options you can choose from vary according to the category chosen.
Complete them as necessary.

4 Click here

3 Complete the relevant options

2 Click a category

Changing fonts and styles

The Spreadsheet module lets you carry out the following actions on cell contents (numbers, text or combinations of both). You can apply:

- a new font

- a new type size

- a font style (*Italic,* Bold, <u>Underlining</u> or ~~Strikethrough~~)

- a colour

Amending the appearance of cell contents

Select the cell(s) whose contents you want to reformat. Pull down the Format menu and click Font and Style. Now follow any of steps 1-4 (as appropriate) below. Finally, carry out step 5.

1 Click a font

2 Type in a type size

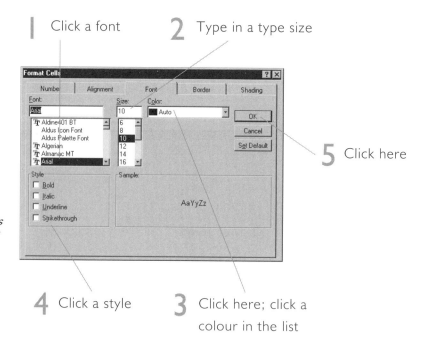

5 Click here

Re step 4 – you can apply multiple styles (e.g. Bold and Italic) if required.

4 Click a style

3 Click here; click a colour in the list

Cell alignment

By default, Works 2000 aligns text to the left of cells, and numbers to the right. However, if you want you can change this.

You can specify alignment under two broad headings: Horizontal and Vertical.

Horizontal alignment

The main options are:

General	the default (see above)
Left	contents are aligned from the left
Right	contents are aligned from the right
Center	contents are centred
Fill	contents are duplicated so that they fill the cell
Center across selection	contents are centred across more than one cell (if you pre-selected a cell range)

Vertical alignment

Available options are:

Top	cell contents align with the top of the cell(s)
Center	contents are centred
Bottom	contents align with the cell bottom

Most of these settings parallel features found in the Word Processor module (and in many other word processors). The difference, however, lies in the fact that in spreadsheets Works 2000 has to align data within the bounds of cells rather than a page. When it aligns text, it often needs to employ its own version of text wrap. See overleaf for more information on this.

By default, when text is too large for the host cell, Works 2000 overflows the surplus into adjacent cells to the right. However, you can opt to have the Spreadsheet module force the text onto separate lines within the original cell. This process is called text wrap.

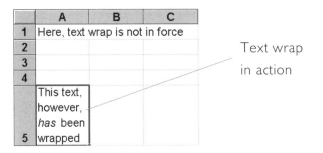

Text wrap
in action

Customising cell alignment & applying text wrap

Select the relevant cell(s). Pull down the Format menu and click Alignment. Now follow any or all of steps 1-3 (as appropriate) below. Finally, carry out step 4:

3 Click a vertical alignment

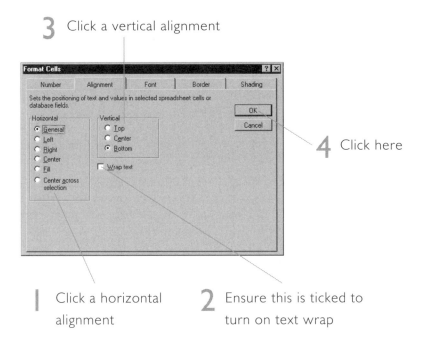

4 Click here

1 Click a horizontal alignment

2 Ensure this is ticked to turn on text wrap

Bordering cells

Bordering cells is a useful technique. Reasons you might want to do this include:

• to emphasise cells or cell ranges, and;

• to create individual lines for graphical effect (especially if gridlines are turned off)

Works 2000 lets you define a border around:

- the perimeter of a selected cell range

- the individual cells within a selected cell range

- specific sides within a cell range

You can customise the border by choosing from a selection of pre-defined border styles. You can also colour the border, if required.

Applying a cell border

First, select the cell range you want to border. Pull down the Format menu and click Border. Now carry out steps 1-2 below. Step 3 is optional. Finally, follow step 4::

Re step 1 – Outline borders the perimeter of the selected cells.

The other options (you can click more than 1) affect individual sides.

1 Click a border – see the HOT TIP

2 Click a line style

If you're setting multiple border options, repeat steps 1-3 as required, before you carry out step 4.

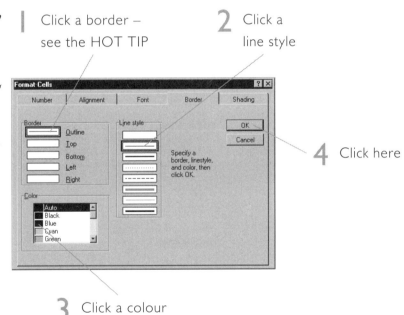

4 Click here

To remove a border, select the relevant cells. Launch the Format Cells dialog with the Border tab active. In the Border section, click the border you want to disable. In the Line style section, click this:

3 Click a colour

Repeat the above until all the borders have been removed. Finally, click OK.

Shading cells

Works 2000 lets you apply the following to cells:

- a pattern

- a foreground colour

- a background colour

You can do any of these singly, or in combination. Interesting effects can be achieved by using foreground colours with coloured backgrounds.

Applying a pattern or background

First, select the cell range you want to shade. Pull down the Format menu and click Shading. Now follow steps 1, 2 and/ or 3 as appropriate. Finally, carry out step 4:

Click a shading or pattern

The Sample area previews how your shading will look.

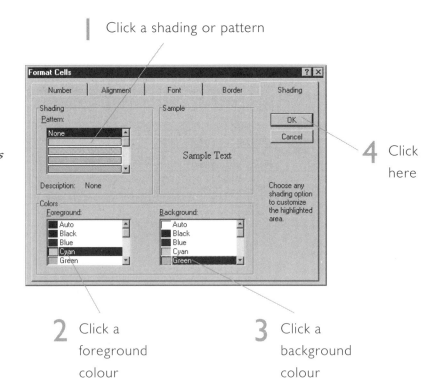

2 Click a foreground colour

3 Click a background colour

4 Click here

AutoFormat

Works 2000 provides a shortcut to the formatting of spreadsheet data: AutoFormat.

AutoFormat consists of 16 pre-defined formatting schemes. These incorporate specific excerpts from the font, number, alignment, border and shading options discussed earlier. You can apply any of these schemes (and their associated formatting) to selected cell ranges with just a few mouse clicks. Doing this saves a lot of time and effort, and the results are dependably professional.

You can undo (reverse) AutoFormats by pressing Ctrl+Z immediately after imposing them.
(This technique also works with most other Spreadsheet editing actions.)

AutoFormat works with most arrangements of spreadsheet data. However, if the effect you achieve isn't what you want, see the DON'T FORGET tip.

Using AutoFormat

First, select the cell range you want to apply an automatic format to. Pull down the Format menu and click AutoFormat. Now carry out steps 1 and 2 below:

2 Click here

The Example field previews how your data will look with the specified AutoFormat.

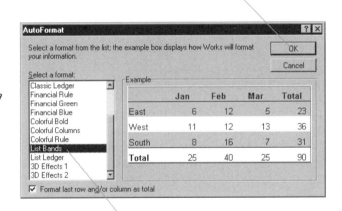

| Click the format you want to apply

Find operations

The Spreadsheet lets you search for and jump to text and/or numbers (in short, any information) in your spreadsheets. This is a particularly useful feature when spreadsheets become large and complex, as they almost invariably do.

In Find operations, you can specify whether Works 2000 searches:

- by columns or rows

- in cells which contain formulas

- in cells which don't contain formulas

Searching for data

Place the mouse pointer at the location in the active spreadsheet from which you want the search to begin. Pull down the Edit menu and click Find. (Or press Ctrl+F.) Now carry out step 1 below, then either of steps 2-3. Finally, carry out step 4:

Type in the data you want to find

4 Click here

If you want to restrict the search to specific cells, select a cell range before you follow steps 1-4.

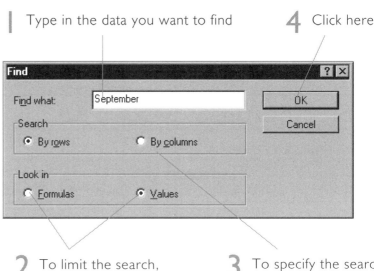

2 To limit the search, click the relevant option

3 To specify the search direction, click the relevant option

Search-and-replace operations

When you search for data, you can also – if you want – have Works 2000 replace it with something else.

Search-and-replace operations can be organised by rows or by columns. However, unlike straight searches, you can't specify whether Works looks in cells which contain formulas or those which don't.

Running a search-and-replace operation

Place the mouse pointer at the location in the active spreadsheet from which you want the search to begin. Pull down the Edit menu and click Replace. Carry out steps 1-3 below. Now do *one* of the following:

— Follow step 4. When Works locates the first search target, carry out step 5 to have it replaced. Repeat this process as often as necessary

— Carry out step 6 to have Works find every target and replace it automatically

If you want to restrict the search-and-replace operation to specific cells, select a cell range before you follow the procedures outlined here.

1 Type in the search data

4 Click here to find the 1st occurrence

5 Click here to replace it

3 To specify the search direction, click the relevant option

2 Type in the replacement data

6 Click here to replace *all* occurrences

Charting – an overview

The Spreadsheet module has comprehensive charting capabilities. You can have it convert selected data into its visual equivalent. To do this, Works 2000 offers 12 chart formats:

Charts make data more attractive, and therefore easier to take in.

- Area
- Bar
- Line
- Pie
- Stacked Line
- X-Y (Scatter)

- Radar
- Combination
- 3-D Area
- 3-D Bar
- 3-D Line
- 3-D Pie

Works 2000 uses a special dialog to make the process of creating charts as easy and convenient as possible.

The illustration below shows a sample 3-D Area chart:

When you create a chart, Works 2000 launches it in a separate Chart Editor window.

You can have as many as 8 charts associated with any spreadsheet.

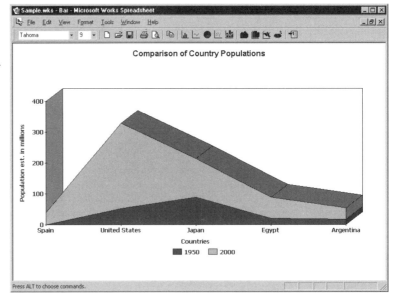

Creating a chart

When you select the data cells, include a row or column of text entries if you want these inserted into the chart as descriptive labels.

Select the cells you want to view as a chart. Pull down the Tools menu and click Create New Chart. Carry out steps 1-3 below. Follow steps 4-6 if you need to set advanced chart options. If you didn't follow steps 4-6, carry out step 7.

| Ensure the Basic Options tab is active

If this is the first time you've created a chart (or if you haven't yet performed step A below) an extra dialog launches before step 1. Do the following:

A Select this   B Click here

Now complete steps 1-6.

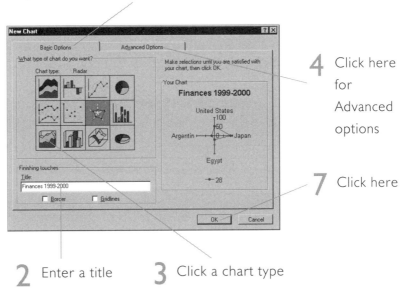

4 Click here for Advanced options

7 Click here

2 Enter a title   3 Click a chart type

5 Complete this section, as appropriate

When you've just created a chart, you may find the effect isn't what you wanted. If so, you can fine-tune the data series it's based on.

Pull down the Edit menu and click Series. In the Edit Series dialog, amend the value and category series, as appropriate. Click OK to redraw the chart.

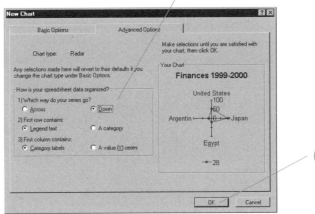

6 Click here

Amending chart formats

Once you've created a chart, you can easily change the underlying chart type. You can also apply a new sub-type.

Each basic chart type has several sub-types (variations) associated with it.

These are unavailable when you first create your chart.

Switch to the chart you want to reformat (if it isn't already open, first follow the procedure under 'Viewing charts' on page 132). Pull down the Format menu and click Chart Type. Follow steps 1-2. If you want to apply a sub-type, carry out 3-5. If you *didn't* follow steps 3-5, follow step 6.

1 Ensure the Basic Types tab is active

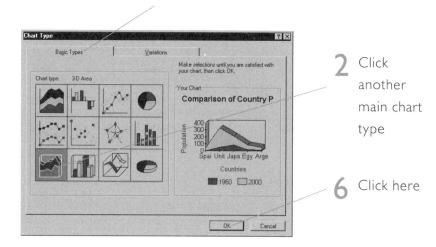

2 Click another main chart type

6 Click here

3 Click the Variations tab

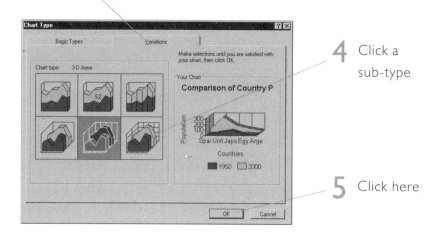

4 Click a sub-type

5 Click here

Reformatting charts

Text which is selected (like all chart objects) is surrounded by handles:

You can reformat charts in the following ways. You can:

- apply a new typeface/type size/font style to text

- apply a new colour/shade to graphic components

Reformatting text

Within the open chart, click the text you want to change. Pull down the Format menu and click Font and Style. Carry out any of steps 1-4, as appropriate. Finally, follow step 5:

The series in a chart are the individual data entries. Below are sample series from a 3D bar chart:

2 Type in a type size

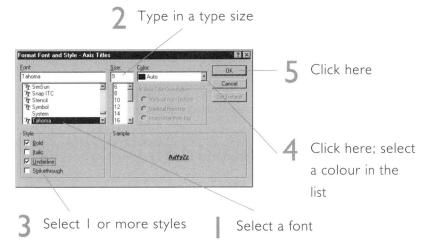

5 Click here

4 Click here; select a colour in the list

1 Select a font

3 Select 1 or more styles

Re step 3 – click Format All instead to apply the changes to all related value series.

Reformatting graphic objects

Double-click the object (e.g. a series) you want to reformat. Carry out step 1 and/or 2 below. Finally, follow step 3.

To close the Format Shading and Color dialog, click this button:

Close

after step 3.

1 Click a colour

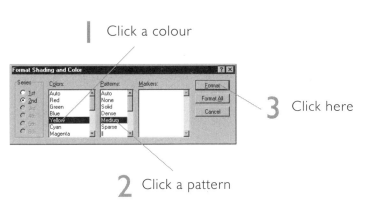

3 Click here

2 Click a pattern

Chart housekeeping

You can't select more than one chart at a time here. To view multiple charts, simply repeat this procedure as often as required.

Viewing charts

A Works 2000 spreadsheet can have a maximum of 8 charts associated with it. To view a chart (when the spreadsheet or another chart is on-screen), pull down the View menu and click Chart. Now do the following:

Click a chart

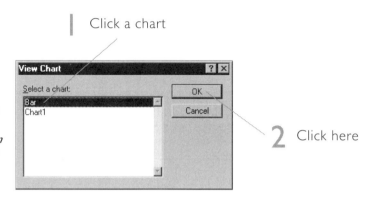

2 Click here

When you've finished working with your chart(s), you can return to the underlying spreadsheet by pulling down the View menu and clicking Spreadsheet.

Deleting charts

If you try to create more than 8 charts for a particular spreadsheet, Works 2000 will refuse to comply. The answer is to delete one or more unwanted charts.

Follow the procedure above to switch to the chart you want to remove. Pull down the Tools menu and click Delete Chart. Now do the following:

Click a chart

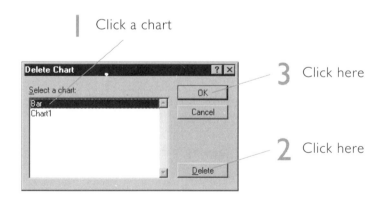

3 Click here

2 Click here

If you want to delete more than one chart, follow steps 1-2 as often as necessary.
Finally, carry out step 3.

After step 3, the Spreadsheet module launches a warning. Do the following:

4 Click here

Page setup – an overview

Making sure your spreadsheets print with the correct page setup can be a complex issue, for the simple reason that most become very extensive with the passage of time (so large, in fact, that in the normal course of things they won't fit onto a single page). Luckily, Works 2000 makes the entire page setup issue easy.

Page setup features you can customise include:

- the paper size

- the page orientation

- the starting page number

- margins

- whether gridlines are printed

- whether row and column headers are printed

Margin settings you can amend are:

— the top margin

— the bottom margin

— the left margin

— the right margin

Additionally, you can set the distance between the top page edge and the top of the header, and the distance between the bottom page edge and the bottom edge of the footer.

When you save your active spreadsheet, all Page Setup settings are automatically saved with it.

Setting size/orientation options

The Spreadsheet module comes with 17 pre-defined paper types which you can apply to your spreadsheets, in either portrait (top-to-bottom) or landscape (sideways on) orientation.

 Portrait orientation

 Landscape orientation

If none of the supplied page definitions is suitable, you can create your own.

Applying a new page size/orientation

Pull down the File menu and click Page Setup. Now carry out step 1 below, followed by steps 2-3 as appropriate. Finally, carry out step 4:

Ensure this tab is active

To create your own paper size, click Custom Size in step 2. Then type in appropriate measurements in the Height & Width fields. Finally, carry out steps 3-4.

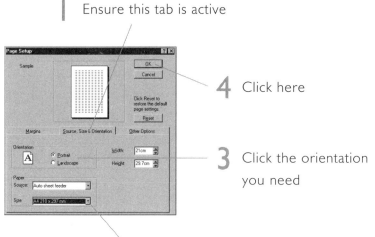

4 Click here

3 Click the orientation you need

2 Click here; click the page size you need in the drop-down list

Setting margin options

The Spreadsheet module lets you set a variety of margin settings. The illustration below shows the main ones:

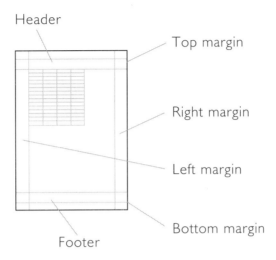

Header
Top margin
Right margin
Left margin
Bottom margin
Footer

Applying new margins

Pull down the File menu and click Page Setup. Now carry out step 1 below, followed by steps 2-3 as appropriate. Finally, carry out step 4:

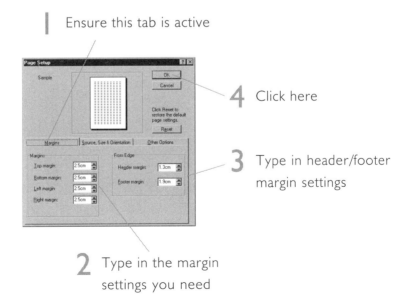

1 Ensure this tab is active

4 Click here

3 Type in header/footer margin settings

2 Type in the margin settings you need

Other page setup options

If you're unsure what column and row headings look like, refer to page 96.

(For how to view gridlines within the spreadsheet itself, see the HOT TIP on page 100.)

You can determine whether gridlines and row/column headings print.

Pull down the File menu and do the following:

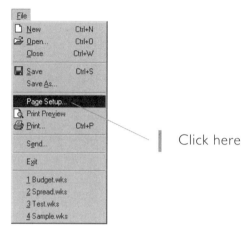

Click here

2 Ensure the Other Options tab is active

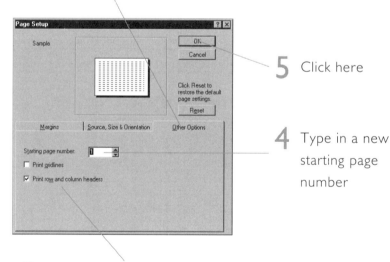

Re step 4 – here, you can set the page number for the first page in your spreadsheet (the default is '1').

5 Click here

4 Type in a new starting page number

3 Select Print gridlines and/or Print row and column headers

Page setup for charts

Most page setup issues for charts are identical to those for spreadsheet data. However, there are differences. The following additional options are available:

Full page   the chart is expanded to fill the
                           page, with its width/height ratio
                           disrupted, if necessary

Full page, keep   the chart is scaled to fit the page,
proportions   but with its width/height ratio
                           unaltered

Screen size   the chart is reduced to the size of
                           your computer screen (so that it
                           occupies roughly 25% of the page)

Customising printed chart sizes

Pull down the File menu and click Page Setup. Now carry out steps 1-3 below:

| Ensure the Other Options tab is active

3 Click here

2 Click a scale option

Using Print Preview

If you want to preview charts, you can use an alternative route. While editing a chart, pull down the View menu and click Display as Printed. Works 2000 now displays the chart in situ, as it will look when printed. You can go on editing the chart in the usual way.

(To return to the normal view, pull down the View menu and click Display as Printed again.)

The Spreadsheet module provides a special view mode called Print Preview. This displays the active spreadsheet (one page at a time) exactly as it will look when printed. Use Print Preview as a final check just before you begin printing.

When you're using Print Preview, you can zoom in or out on the active page. What you can't do, however, is:

• display more than one page at a time

• edit or revise the active spreadsheet or chart (in the case of charts, however, see the HOT TIP for a work-round)

Launching Print Preview

Pull down the File menu and click Print Preview. This is the result:

A preview of a chart

This is a Radar chart. For how to apply this and other chart types, see page 130.

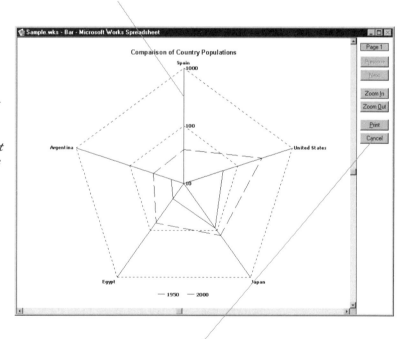

You can use a keyboard shortcut to leave Print Preview mode and return to your spreadsheet or chart. Simply press Esc.

Click Cancel to leave Print Preview

Zooming in or out in Print Preview

There are two methods you can use here.

Using the mouse
Do the following:

Move the mouse pointer over the page (it changes to a magnifying glass)

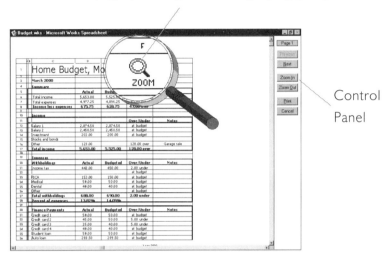

Control Panel

Repeat step 2 to increase the magnification even more. (Doing so again, however, returns it to the original level.)

2 Left-click once to increase the magnification

Using the Control Panel
Launch Print Preview. Then carry out the following actions:

Depending on the current level of magnification, one of the Zoom buttons may be greyed out, and therefore unavailable.

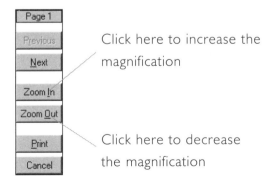

Click here to increase the magnification

Click here to decrease the magnification

Changing pages in Print Preview

Although you can only view one page at a time in Print Preview mode, you can step backwards and forwards through the spreadsheet as often as necessary.

There are three methods you can use (in descending order of usefulness).

Using the Control Panel

Carry out the following actions:

Depending on your location within the document (and the number of pages), one of these buttons may be greyed out, and therefore unavailable.

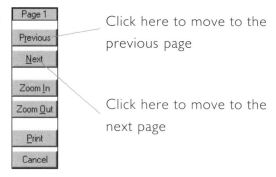

Click here to move to the previous page

Click here to move to the next page

Using the keyboard

You can use the following keyboard shortcuts:

In a magnified page view, the Page Up and Page Down keys move through the current page.

Page Up	Moves to the previous page (unavailable within a magnified page view)
Page Down	Moves to the next page (unavailable within a magnified page view)
Up cursor	Within a magnified view of a page, moves towards the top of the page
Down cursor	Within a magnified view of a page, moves towards the base of the page

Using the scrollbars

When you're working with a magnified view of a page, use the vertical and/or horizontal scrollbars (using standard Windows techniques) to move up or down within the page.

Printing spreadsheet data

When you print your data, you can specify:

- the number of copies you want printed

- whether you want the copies 'collated'. This is the process whereby Works 2000 prints one full copy at a time. For instance, if you're printing five copies of a 12-page spreadsheet, Works prints pages 1-12 of the first copy, followed by pages 1-12 of the second and pages 1-12 of the third... and so on.

- which pages you want printed

- the printer you want to use (if you have more than one installed on your system)

You can 'mix and match' these, as appropriate.

Starting a print run

Open the spreadsheet containing the data you want to print. Then pull down the File menu and click Print. Perform any of steps 1-4. Then carry out step 5 to begin printing:

If you need to adjust your printer's internal settings before you initiate printing, click Properties. Then refer to your printer's manual.

If this is the first time you've printed anything (or if you haven't yet performed step A below) an extra dialog launches before step 1. Do the following:

A Select this   B Click here

Now complete steps 1-6.

Click Draft quality printing to have your spreadsheet print with minimal formatting.

1 Click here; select a printer from the list

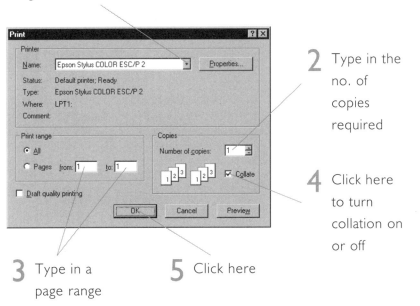

2 Type in the no. of copies required

4 Click here to turn collation on or off

3 Type in a page range

5 Click here

Printing – the fast track approach

In earlier topics, we've looked at how to customise print options to meet varying needs and spreadsheet sizes. However, the Spreadsheet module – like the Word Processor – recognises that there will be times when you won't need this level of complexity. There are occasions when you'll merely want to print out your work (often for proofing purposes):

- bypassing the Print dialog, and;

- with the current print settings applying

For this reason, Works provides a method which is much quicker and easier to use.

Printing with the default print options

First, open the spreadsheet you want to print. Ensure your printer is ready. Make sure the Toolbar is visible. (If it isn't, pull down the View menu and click Toolbar). Now do the following:

Click here

The active spreadsheet starts to print straightaway

The Database

This chapter gives you the basics of using the Database. You'll learn how to work with data and formulas, and how to move around in databases (including the use of Zoom). You'll also discover how to select and locate data, and apply formatting to make it more visually effective. Finally, you'll generate reports, then customise page layout/printing.

Covers

The Database screen | 144

Creating your first database | 145

Entering and modifying data | 146

Using Database views | 149

Moving around in databases | 151

Using Zoom | 153

Selection techniques | 154

Formulas and functions | 156

Working with fields/records | 160

Fills | 163

Formatting | 165

Find and search-and-replace operations | 169

Page setup | 171

Report creation | 175

Print Preview and printing | 176

Chapter Four

The Database screen

Below is a detailed illustration of a typical Database screen.

Title bar   Menu bar

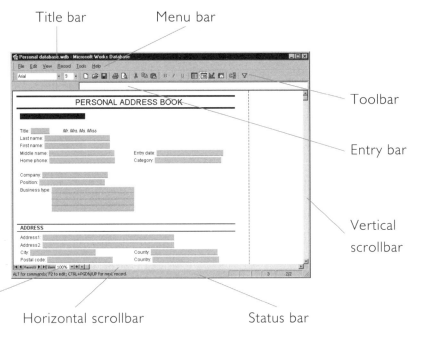

Toolbar

Entry bar

Vertical scrollbar

Here, the database is displaying in Form view. For more information on Database views, see pages 149-150.

This is the Zoom Area: The screen components here are used to adjust magnification levels. See page 153.

Horizontal scrollbar   Status bar

Some of these – e.g. the rulers and scrollbars – are standard to just about all programs which run under Windows. One – the Toolbar – can be hidden, if required.

Specifying whether the Toolbar displays

Pull down the View menu and do the following:

The tick signifies that the Toolbar is currently visible.

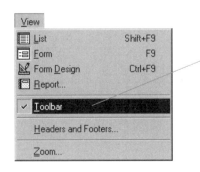

Click here to view or hide the Toolbar

Creating your first database

To start using the Task Launcher to create a new Database document, follow the procedures in the DON'T FORGET tip on page 12. Then perform steps 1-4 here.

Unlike the Word Processor and Spreadsheet modules, the Database *doesn't* create a new blank document immediately after you've launched the module from within the Task Launcher. Instead, you have to complete several dialogs first. Do the following:

If this is the first time you've created a database (or if you haven't yet performed step A below) an extra dialog launches before step 1. Do the following:

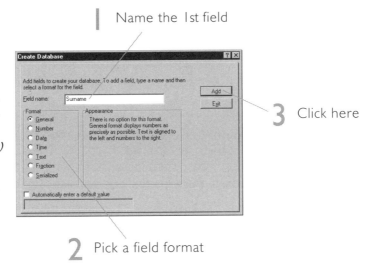

Name the 1st field

3 Click here

2 Pick a field format

A Select this

B Click here

Now complete steps 1-4.

After you've followed step 3, Works 2000 reproduces the same dialog so that you can create the second field. Repeat the above procedures as often as necessary. When you've defined your final field, do the following:

Database fields are single columns of information (in List view) or spaces for the insertion of information (in Form view).

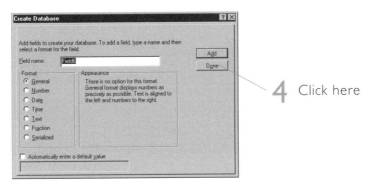

4 Click here

Entering data

When you've created a database, you can begin entering data immediately. You can enter the following basic data types:

- numbers

- text

- functions

- formulas (combinations of numbers, text and functions)

In List view, records are shown as single rows. In Form view, only one record displays on-screen at any given time.
For more information on Database views, see pages 149-150.

You enter data into 'fields'. Fields are organised into 'records'. Records are whole units of related information.

To understand this, we'll take a specific example. In an address book, the categories under which information is entered (e.g. Last name, First Name, Home Phone) are fields, while each person whose details are entered into the database constitutes one record. This is shown in the next illustration:

This is List view. List view is suitable for the mass insertion of data (more than 1 record is visible at a time). However, you can also enter data in Form view.

Fields

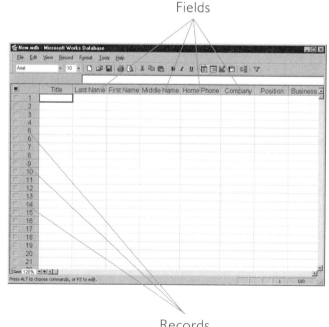

Records

...cont'd

You can insert the Euro symbol into databases. Fonts which support this include:

- *Arial*
- *Courier New*
- *Impact*
- *Tahoma, and;*
- *Times New Roman*

To insert the Euro symbol, press the Num Lock key on your keyboard. Hold down Alt and press 0128 (consecutively). Release Alt and turn off Num Lock.

Here, the Zoom level has been increased to make the data more visible.
For how to do this, see page 153.

Although you can enter data *directly* into a database field (by simply clicking in it and typing it in), there's another method you can use which is often easier. Like the Spreadsheet module, the Database provides a special screen component known as the Entry bar.

In the illustration below, two fields in the first record have been completed.

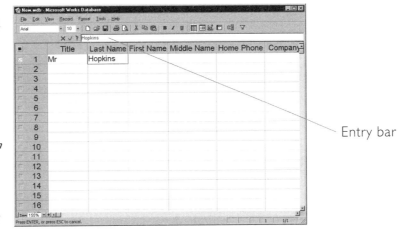

Entry bar

Entering data via the Entry bar

Click the field you want to insert data into. Then click the Entry bar. Type in the data. Then follow step 1 below. If you decide not to proceed with the operation, follow step 2 instead:

You can use a keyboard route to confirm operations in the Entry bar. Simply press Return. (Or press Esc to cancel them.)

Click here

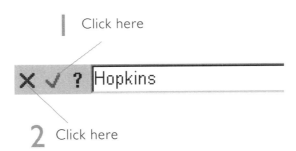

2 Click here

Modifying existing data

You can amend the contents of a field in two ways:

- via the Entry bar

- from within the field itself

When you use either of these methods, the Database enters a special state known as Edit Mode.

Amending existing data using the Entry bar

Click the field whose contents you want to change. Then click in the Entry bar. Make the appropriate revisions and/or additions. Then press Return. The relevant field is updated.

Amending existing data internally

Click the field whose contents you want to change. Press F2. Make the appropriate revisions and/or additions *within the field*. Then press Return.

The illustration below shows our new database, in Form view.

This is Form view before any formatting enhancements have been applied – for an idea of what a more developed Form view looks like, see the appropriate illustration on the facing page.

This is the first record in our database.

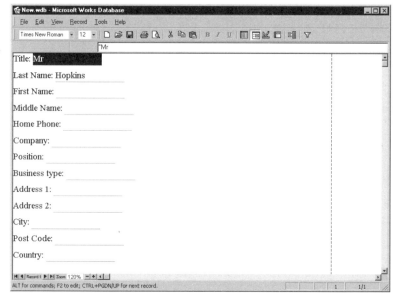

Using Database views

The Database module provides two principal views:

List

Pictures and most formatting components do not display in List view.

List view presents your data in a grid structure reminiscent of the Spreadsheet module, with the columns denoting fields and the rows individual records.

Use List view for bulk data entry or comparison.

Form

Pictures and formatting display in Form view (although you can only initiate or modify them in Form Design view)

Form view limits the display to one record at a time, while presenting it in a way which is more visual and therefore easier on the eye. The basis of this view is the 'form', the underlying database layout which you can customise in Form Design view.

In many circumstances, Form view provides the best way to interact with your database.

Form Design view is a subset of Form view. (For how to use Form Design view, see pages 165-168).

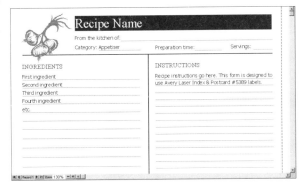

A database in Form view...

There are two further view modes: Report (see page 175) and Print Preview (see pages 176-178).

A database in List view...

You can use three methods to switch to another view.

The menu approach...
Pull down the View menu and do the following:

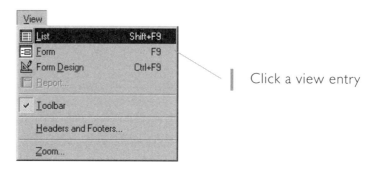

Click a view entry

If the Toolbar isn't currently on-screen, pull down the View menu and click Toolbar.

The Toolbar approach...
Refer to the Toolbar. Now click one of the following:

Form view

Form Design view

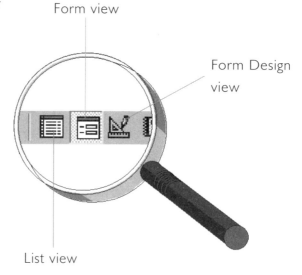

You can also use the following keyboard shortcuts:

F9	*Form view*
Shift+F9	*List view*
Ctrl+F9	*Form Design view*

List view

Moving around in databases

Databases can quickly become very large. The Database module provides several techniques you can use to find your way round.

Using the scrollbars

Use any of the following methods:

1. To scroll quickly to another record (in List view) or to another field (in Form view), drag the scroll box along the Vertical scrollbar until you reach it

2. To move one window to the right or left, click to the left or right of the scroll box in the Horizontal scrollbar

3. To move one window up or down, click above or below the scroll box in the Vertical scrollbar

4. To move up or down by one record (in List view) or one field (in Form view), click the arrows in the Vertical scrollbar

5. To move left or right by one field, click the arrows in the Horizontal scrollbar

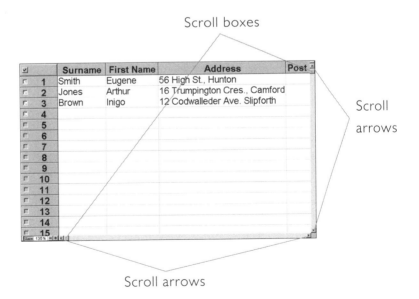

Scroll boxes

Scroll arrows

Scroll arrows

Using the keyboard

You can use the following techniques:

1. In List view, use the cursor keys to move one field left, right, up or down. In Form or Form Design views, use the up and left cursor keys to move one field up, or the down and right keys to move one field down

2. Press Home to jump to the first field in the active record, or End to move to the last

3. Press Ctrl+Home to move to the first record in the open database, or Ctrl+End to move to the last

4. Press Page Up or Page Down to move up or down by one screen

5. In Form or Form Design views, press Ctrl+Page Down to move to the next record, or Ctrl+Page Up to move to the previous one

Using the Go To dialog

You can use a keyboard shortcut to launch the Go To dialog. Simply press F5, or Ctrl+G.

The Database provides a special dialog which you can use to specify precise field or record destinations.

In any view, pull down the Edit menu and click Go To. Now carry out step 1 OR 2 below. Finally, follow step 3.

2 Type in a record number

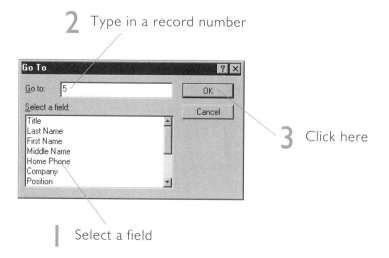

3 Click here

Select a field

Using Zoom

The ability to vary the level of magnification in the Database module is very useful. Sometimes, it's helpful to 'zoom out' (i.e. decrease the magnification) so that you can take an overview; at other times, you'll need to 'zoom in' (increase the magnification) to work in greater detail. Works 2000 makes this process easy and convenient.

You can change magnification levels in the Database module:

• with the use of the Zoom Area

• with the Zoom dialog

See the screen illustration on page 144 for more information on where to find the Zoom Area.

Using the Zoom Area

You can use the Zoom Area (at the base of the screen) to alter zoom levels with the minimum of effort. Carry out step 1 or 2, or steps 3-4, as appropriate:

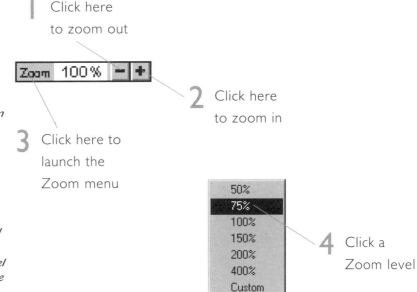

1 Click here to zoom out

2 Click here to zoom in

3 Click here to launch the Zoom menu

4 Click a Zoom level

Re step 4 – clicking Custom produces the Zoom dialog (you can also launch this by selecting Zoom in the View menu).
In the dialog, do one of the following:

• *select a preset Zoom level (e.g. 75% or 200%), or;*
• *enter your own Zoom level in the Custom field (in the range 40-1000%)*

Finally, click OK.

Selection techniques in List view

Before you can carry out any editing operations on fields or records in the Database module, you have to select them first. The available selection techniques vary according to whether you're currently using List, Form or Form Design view.

In List view, follow any of the techniques below:

Using the mouse

To select a single field — Simply click in it

To select multiple fields — Click the field in the top left-hand corner; hold down the mouse button and drag over the fields you want to highlight. Release the mouse button

With the exception of the first, selected fields are filled with black.

To select one record — Click the record number

To select several records — Hold down Shift as you click the record numbers

To select the whole of the active database in List view, press Ctrl+Shift+F8.

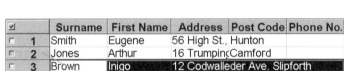

☑		Surname	First Name	Address	Post Code	Phone No.
☐	1	Smith	Eugene	56 High St., Hunton		
☐	2	Jones	Arthur	16 Trumpin Camford		
☐	3	Brown	Inigo	12 Codwalleder Ave. Slipforth		

Record numbers

Using the keyboard

Pressing F8 makes the Database enter Selection Mode. When it does, the following displays in the Status bar:

Selection Mode is in force

To select multiple fields — Position the insertion point in the first field. Press F8. Use the cursor keys to extend the selection area. Press F8 when you've finished

To select a whole record — Position the insertion point in the record. Press Ctrl+F8

To select a whole field — Position the insertion point in the field. Press Shift+F8

Selection techniques in forms

Note that some of the techniques discussed here (they're clearly marked) will only work in Form Design view.

These arrow buttons can be found in the bottom left-hand corner of the Form and Form Design view screens.

Using the mouse

To select a single field   Simply click in it.

To select multiple fields   Hold down Ctrl as you click in successive fields (you must be in Form Design view to do this).

To select one record   Click any of the following:

To previous record   To final record

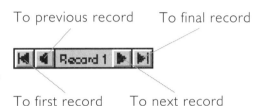

To first record   To next record

To select multiple field names or inserted pictures   In Form Design view, hold down Ctrl as you click successive objects.

You can insert clip art into databases, but only in Form Design view:

Ensure no item is selected. Pull down the Insert menu and click Clip Art. Use the Clip Gallery to locate and insert an image (for help with this, see pages 66-67).

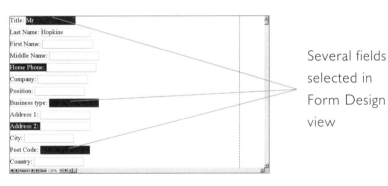

Several fields selected in Form Design view

Using the keyboard

To select a field   Use the cursor keys to position the insertion point in the relevant field

To select a record   Press Ctrl+Page Up or Ctrl+Page Down until the record you want is displayed

Formulas – an overview

You can insert formulas into Database fields. Formulas in the Database module work in much the same way as in the Spreadsheet. However, there are fewer applications for them.

Database formulas serve two principal functions:

- to ensure that the same entry appears in a given field throughout every record in a database

- to return a value based on the contents of multiple additional fields

The formula/ function appears in the Entry bar:

Look at the next illustration:

For the NOW() function to return a date as its result, the host field must have had the Date number format applied to it – see page 160.

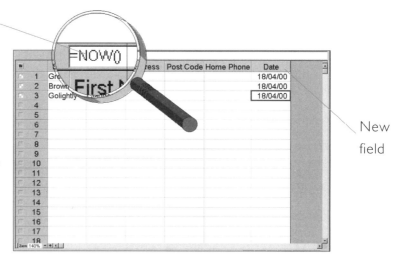

New field

Here, an extra field has been added (see page 160 for how to do this) and a formula (in this case, consisting entirely of a function) inserted. The function:

=NOW()

inserts the current system date in the Date field within every record.

Inserting a formula

As in the Spreadsheet module, all Database formulas must begin with an equals sign. This is usually followed by a permutation of the following:

Arguments (e.g. field references) relating to functions are always contained in brackets.

- one or more operands (in the case of the Database module, field names)

- a function (e.g. AVG – returns the Average)

- an arithmetical operator (+, –, /, * and ^)

The Database supports a very wide assortment of functions. For how to insert functions, refer to pages 158-159.

The arithmetical operators are (in the order in which they appear in the bulleted list above):

plus, minus, divide, multiply and *exponential*.

There are two ways to enter formulas:

Entering a formula directly into the field
Click the field into which you want to insert a formula. Then type =, followed by your formula. When you've finished defining the formula, press Return.

The Entry bar method is usually the most convenient.

Entering a formula into the Entry bar
Click the field in which you want to insert a formula. Then click in the Entry bar. Type =, followed by your formula. When you've finished defining the formula, press Return or:

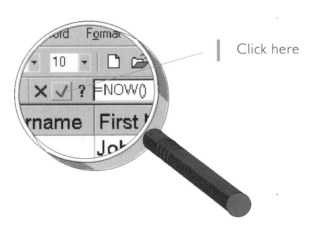

Click here

Database functions

In many ways, the Database module's implementation of functions parallels that of the Spreadsheet module. However, there is one important difference: you can't use Easy Calc to insert them. Instead, you have to do so manually. Luckily, though, the inbuilt HELP system provides assistance.

Using HELP before you insert a function

Pull down the Help menu and click Contents. Now do the following:

After step 4, click a specific function. Works 2000 now launches a dedicated HELP window which tells you how to apply the relevant function:

HELP with the Date function

To close the HELP window, click this button:

in the top right-hand corner.

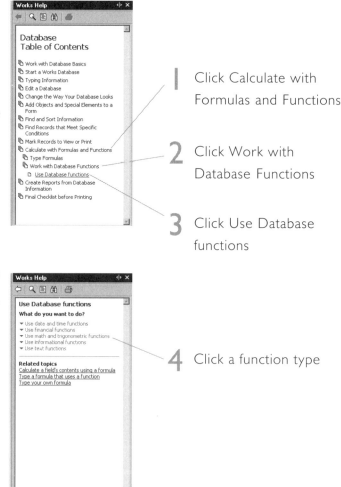

1 Click Calculate with Formulas and Functions

2 Click Work with Database Functions

3 Click Use Database functions

4 Click a function type

Inserting a function

There are two ways to insert functions:

Entering a function directly into the field

1 Click the field into which you want to insert the function

2 Type = followed by the function itself – e.g. =NOW()

3 Don't forget to include any arguments – see the tip

4 Press Enter

Re step 3 – as an example, if you're entering the AVG function (which returns the average of selected fields), type in the field details (arguments) e.g. to average fields called Week1 and Week2, type:

=AVG(Week1,Week2)

Entering a function into the Entry bar

1 Click the field into which you want to insert the function

2 Click in the Entry bar; type = followed by the function itself

3 Don't forget to include any arguments – see the tip

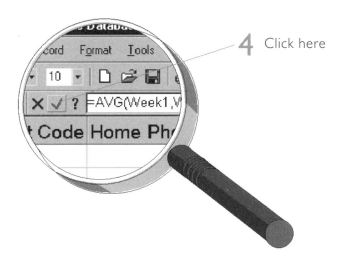

4 Click here

Inserting fields

You can add one or more blank fields to the active database, from Form Design (but not Form) or List view.

Adding a field in Form Design view

If you're not already in Form Design view, pull down the View menu and click Form Design. Click where you want the new field inserted. Pull down the Insert menu and click Field. Do the following:

Re step 2 – most of the number formats you can choose from are identical to those used in the Spreadsheet (see page 119 – especially the HOT TIP – for more information).

Name the new field

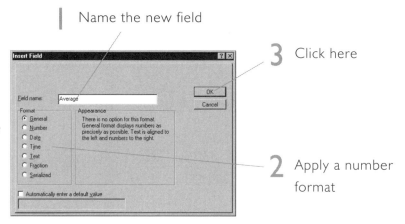

3 Click here

2 Apply a number format

Adding one or more fields in List view

If you're not currently in List view, pull down the View menu and click List. Click in the field (column) next to which you want the new field(s) added. Pull down the Record menu and click Insert Field. In the sub-menu, click Before or After, as appropriate.

The Insert Field dialog launches. Follow steps 1-2 above, then click the Add button. The dialog now changes. Do *either* of the following:

Repeat B. as often as necessary to add as many additional fields as required.

A.   click Done to add the single field and close the dialog, or;

B.   carry out steps 1-2 again (then click Add) to add a further field

If you carried out B., click Done when you've added the correct number of new fields.

Inserting records

You can add one or more blank records to the active database, from within either Form (but not Form Design) or List view.

See pages 151-152 for how to jump to the relevant record.

Adding a record in Form view

If you're not already in Form view, pull down the View menu and click Form. Go to the record before which you want the new record to appear. Pull down the Record menu and click Insert Record.

Adding a record in List view

If you're not currently in List view, pull down the View menu and click List. Click in the record above which you want the new record added. Pull down the Record menu and click Insert Record.

If you select more than one existing record in List view (by holding down Shift as you click the relevant row headings), Works 2000 inserts the equivalent number of new records.

To hide one record in Form view, go to it. In List view, however, select one or more records. Now in either case pull down the Record menu and click Hide Record.

To make all records visible again, pull down the Record menu and click Show All Records.

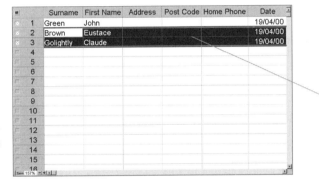

Preparing to add two new records in List view...

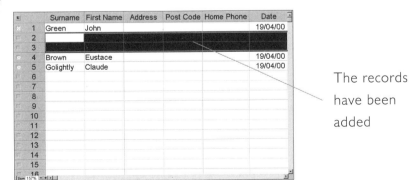

The records have been added

Amending record/field sizes

In Form or List view, you can sort database data alpha-numerically.

Pull down the Record menu and click Sort Records. If the First-time Help dialog appears, (optionally) select Don't display this message in the future. Click OK. In the Sort Records dialog, click the arrow to the right of the Sort by field and select the field you want to sort by. Click Ascending or Descending.

(If you also want to sort by subsidiary fields, complete the above procedures for either – or both – Then by fields.)

Finally, click OK.

Sooner or later, you'll find it necessary to change the dimensions of fields or records within List view. This necessity arises when there is too much data to display adequately. You can enlarge or shrink single or multiple fields/records.

Changing record height

To change one record's height, click the record number. If you want to change multiple records, hold down Shift and click the appropriate extra numbers. Then pull down the Format menu and click Record Height. Carry out the following steps:

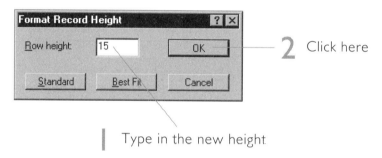

2 Click here

Type in the new height

Changing field widths

To change one field's width, click the field heading. If you want to change multiple fields, hold down Shift and click the appropriate extra headings. Then pull down the Format menu and click Field Width. Now do the following:

Works 2000 has a useful 'best fit' feature. Simply click Best Fit in either dialog to have the record(s) or field(s) adjust themselves automatically to their contents.

(You can also achieve this by double-clicking the relevant column or row heading in List view.)

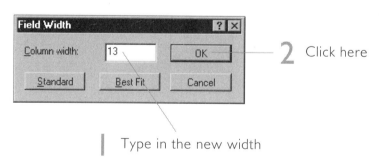

2 Click here

Type in the new width

Working with fills

In List view, you can have the contents of a selected field entry automatically copied into other field entries or records.

Use this technique to save time and effort.

Duplicating a field entry

Click the field entry whose contents you want to duplicate. Then move the mouse pointer over the appropriate border. Click and hold down the button; drag the border over the field entries or records into which you want the contents inserted. Release the button.

Here, the contents of the Home Phone field in record I will be copied into the same field in records 2-3

Now pull down the Edit menu and click Fill Right or Fill Down, as appropriate.

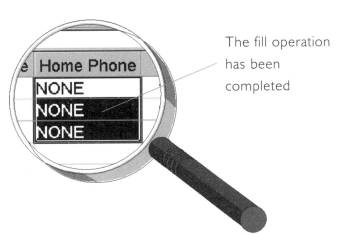

The fill operation has been completed

Working with fill series

You can spell-check database contents. To do this, press F7.
Complete the Spelling dialog in line with steps 1-4 on page 59 (the dialog is rather different, but the procedures are basically the same).

You can also carry out fills which *extrapolate* field entry contents over the specified entries. Look at the next illustration:

The start of a series

Re step 2 – the step value sets the rate by which the series progresses. Use plus numbers for increments, minus numbers for decrements.
For example, setting '-2' in this instance would produce the following series:

• *November, September, July, May, March, January (and so on...)*

whereas '3' would give:

• *April, July, October, January (and so on...)*

If (as here) you wanted to insert progressive month names in successive field entries, you could do so manually. But there's a much easier way. You can have Works do it for you.

Creating a series

Type in the first element(s) of the series in 1 or more consecutive fields. Select all the fields (including those into which you want the series extended). Pull down the Edit menu and click Fill Series. Now do the following:

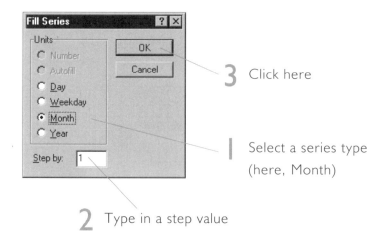

3 Click here

I Select a series type (here, Month)

2 Type in a step value

This is the result of applying the series on the right:

The completed series

Changing fonts and styles

You can apply any of these formatting enhancements from within List or Form Design views. Note, however, that the results are independent – e.g. you can colour the same field red in Form Design view and blue in List view.

The Database module lets you carry out the following actions on field contents (numbers, text or combinations of both). You can:

- apply a new font

- apply a new type size

- apply a font style (*Italic,* Bold, <u>Underlining</u> or ~~Strikethrough~~)

- apply a colour

Amending the appearance of field contents

Select the data you want to reformat. Pull down the Format menu and click Font and Style. Now follow any of steps 1-4, as appropriate. Finally, carry out step 5.

1 Select a font

2 Type in a type size

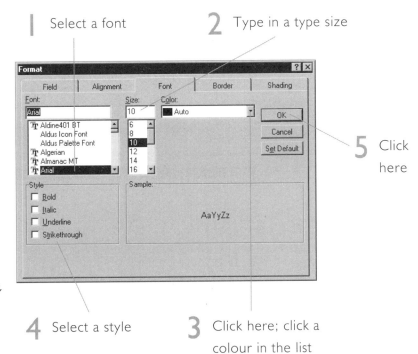

5 Click here

Re step 4 – you can apply multiple styles, if you want.

4 Select a style

3 Click here; click a colour in the list

Aligning field contents

You can apply the following alignments to field entries:

Horizontal alignment

You can carry out any of these from within List or Form Design views. Note, however, that the full alignment options are only available within List view.

General	the default (text to the left, numbers to the right)
Left	contents are aligned from the left
Right	contents are aligned from the right
Center	contents are centred

Vertical alignment

Top	contents align with the top of the field(s)
Center	contents are centred
Bottom	contents align with the base of the field(s)

Customising alignment & applying text wrap

Select the relevant field(s). Pull down the Format menu and click Alignment. Now follow any or all of steps 1-3, as appropriate. Finally, carry out step 4.

This is the List view version of the dialog.

Select a horizontal alignment

Re step 3 – select Wrap text in List view to have any surplus text within a field forced onto separate lines within the field.

(Alternatively, in Form Design view select Slide to left to have Works 2000 change the field height to accommodate text.)

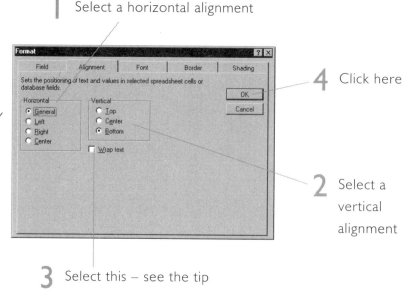

4 Click here

2 Select a vertical alignment

3 Select this – see the tip

Bordering fields

In List view, you can define a border around:

You can border fields in Form Design view, too. However, you can only create perimeter borders.

- the perimeter of selected field(s)

- the individual fields *within* a group of selected fields

- specific field sides

You can customise the border by choosing from a selection of pre-defined border styles. You can also colour it, if required.

Applying a field border

First, click the heading(s) of the field(s) you want to border. Pull down the Format menu and click Border. Now carry out steps 1 and 2 below. Step 3 is optional. (If you're setting multiple border options, repeat steps 1-3 as required). Finally, carry out step 4:

Re step 1 – Outline (unavailable in List view) borders the perimeter of the selected field(s). The other options (you can click more than 1) are only available in Form Design view and affect individual sides.

1 Select the extent of the border (see the HOT TIP)

4 Click here

2 Select a border style

3 Click here; in the list, select a border colour

Shading fields

In List view, you can apply the following to fields:

- a pattern

- a foreground colour

- a background colour

You can apply these effects in Form Design view, too. Note, however, that if no fields have been pre-selected they apply to the whole of the form (and the dialog below is slightly different).

You can do any of these singly, or in combination. Interesting effects can be achieved by using foreground colours with coloured backgrounds.

Applying a pattern or background

First, select the heading(s) of the field(s) you want to shade. Pull down the Format menu and click Shading. Now carry out step 1 below. Follow step 2 and/or 3 as appropriate. Finally, carry out step 4:

Select a shading or pattern

The Sample field previews how your shading will look.

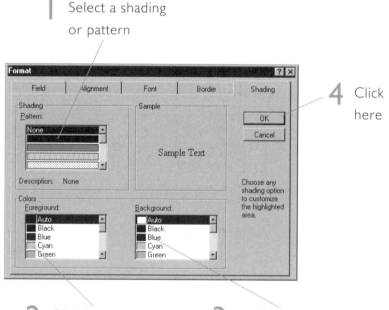

4 Click here

2 Click here; select a foreground colour

3 Click here; select a background colour

Find operations

The Database module lets you search for text and/or numbers. There are two basic options. You can:

- have the first matching record display

- view all records which contain the specified text or numbers

Searching for data

Pull down the Edit menu and click Find. Now carry out step 1 below, then *either* step 2 or 3. Finally, carry out step 4:

Type in the data you want to find

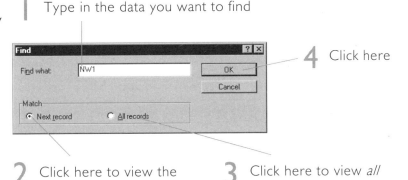

4 Click here

2 Click here to view the first matching record

3 Click here to view *all* matching records

Showing all records again

If you followed step 3 above, Works 2000 will only display matching records (other records in your database are inaccessible). To show all records again, pull down the Record menu and do the following:

1 Click here

2 Click here

Search-and-replace operations

When you search for data, you can also – if you want – have Works 2000 replace it with something else.

You can specify the following search directions:

You can only carry out search-and-replace operations in List view.

Records   the search is left-to-right

Fields   the search is top-to-bottom

Running a search-and-replace operation

Pull down the Edit menu and click Replace. Carry out steps 1-3 below. Now do *one* of the following:

You can also use a keyboard shortcut to launch the Replace dialog. Simply press Ctrl+H.

—   Follow step 4. When Works locates the first search target, carry out step 5 to have it replaced. Repeat this process as often as necessary.

—   Carry out step 6 to have Works find *every* target and replace it automatically.

1 Type in the data you want to find

4 Click here to find the 1st occurrence

5 Click here

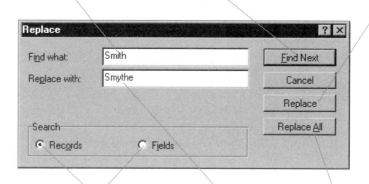

3 To specify the search direction, click the relevant option

2 Type in the replacement data

6 Click here to replace *all* occurrences

Page setup – an overview

When you come to print out your database, it's important to ensure the page setup is correct. Luckily, Works makes this easy.

See the HOT TIP on page 174 for extra page setup features which are only available in Form and Form Design views.

Page setup features you can customise (in List and Form views) include:

*   the paper size

*   the page orientation

*   the starting page number

*   margins

*   whether gridlines are printed

*   whether record and field headings are printed

Field headings

This is a section of a database viewed in Print Preview mode – see pages 176-178.

	Surname	First Name	Address	Post Code	Phone No.
1	Smith	Eugene	56 High St., Hunton		
2	Jones	Arthur	16 TrumpingCamford		
3	Brown	Inigo	12 Codwalleder Ave. Slipforth		
4	Smith				

Record headings

Margin settings you can amend are:

— the top margin

— the bottom margin

— the left margin

— the right margin

When you save your active database, all page setup settings are saved with it.

Setting size/orientation options

The Database module comes with 17 pre-defined paper types which you can apply to your databases, in either portrait (top-to-bottom) or landscape (sideways on) orientation.

Portrait orientation

Landscape orientation

If none of the supplied page definitions is suitable, you can create your own.

Applying a new page size/orientation

Pull down the File menu and click Page Setup. Now carry out step 1 below, followed by steps 2-3 as appropriate. Finally, carry out step 4:

To create your own paper size, click Custom Size in step 2. Then type in the relevant measurements in the Height & Width fields. Finally, carry out steps 3-4.

1 Ensure this tab is active

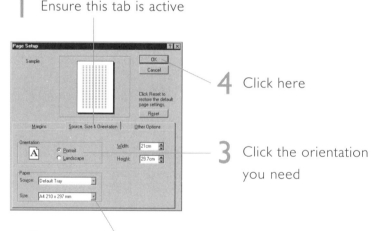

4 Click here

3 Click the orientation you need

2 Click here; click the page size you need in the drop-down list

Setting margin options

The Database module lets you set a variety of margin settings. The illustration below shows the main ones:

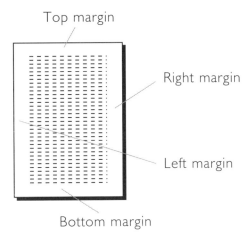

Top margin

Right margin

Left margin

Bottom margin

Applying new margins

Pull down the File menu and click Page Setup. Now carry out step 1-3 below:

1 Ensure this tab is active

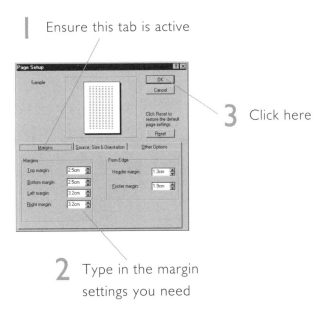

3 Click here

2 Type in the margin settings you need

Other page setup options

You can determine whether gridlines and record/field headers print. These are demonstrated below:

Magnified view of field heading

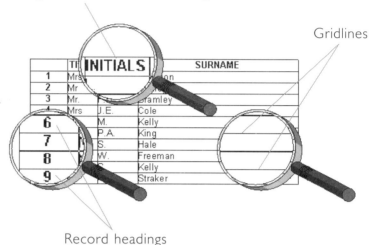

Gridlines

Record headings

You can also set the page number for the first page in your database – the default is '1'.

To apply a new start number, type it into the Starting page number: field.

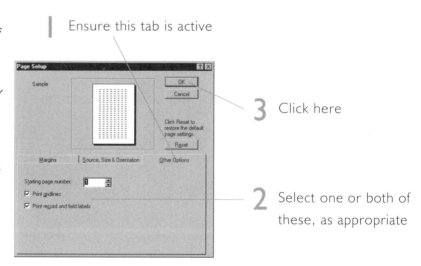

Re step 2 – if you launch this dialog from within Form or Form Design view, you can select the following instead:

Print field lines	enables lines between fields
Page breaks between records	records are separated by page breaks
All items	all fields print
Field entries only	only field entries print

You can also specify a gap between records (by entering it in the Space between records field).

Printing gridlines and record/field headings

Pull down the File menu and click Page Setup. Now carry out step 1 below, followed by step 2 as appropriate. Finally, carry out step 3:

Ensure this tab is active

3 Click here

2 Select one or both of these, as appropriate

Report creation

A Select this   B Click here

Now complete steps 1-4.

You can use a special Database feature – ReportCreator – to compile a report according to the criteria you set. When you use ReportCreator, you can specify:

- how the report is named (you can also allocate a working title/heading)

- which fields are included

- the order in which fields are arranged ('sorting')

- which records are included ('filtering')

When a report has been generated, Works 2000 stores it in a special view mode called Report Definition. This resembles List view (but has labelled rows, not numbered records).

Creating a report

Pull down the Tools menu and click ReportCreator. Do the following:

1 Name the report

2 Click here

3 Type in a heading   Tabs

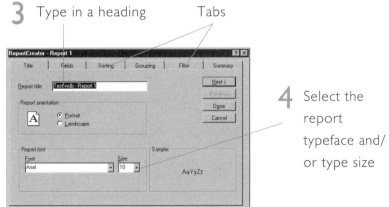

4 Select the report typeface and/ or type size

Using Print Preview

To view an existing report in Print Preview, pull down the View menu and click Report. In the View Report dialog, double-click a report.

The Database module provides a special view mode called Print Preview. This displays the active database (one page at a time) exactly as it will look when printed. Use Print Preview as a final check just before you begin printing.

When you're using Print Preview, you can zoom in or out on the active page. What you can't do, however, is:

- display more than one page at a time

- edit or revise the active document

Launching Print Preview

Pull down the File menu and click Print Preview. This is the result:

You can use a keyboard shortcut to leave Print Preview mode and return to your database. Simply press Esc.

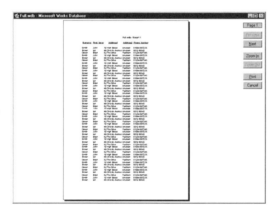

A database in List view, viewed in Print Preview

Here, the Zoom level has been increased – see the facing page.

A database in Form view, viewed in Print Preview

Zooming in or out in Print Preview

There are two methods you can use here.

Using the mouse
Do the following:

Move the mouse pointer over the page (it changes to a magnifying glass)

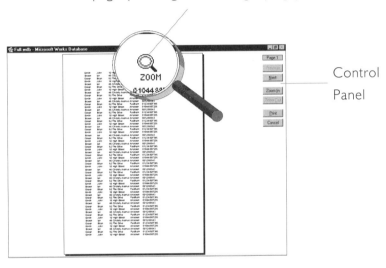

Control Panel

Repeat step 2 to increase the magnification even more. (Doing so again, however, returns it to the original level.)

2 Left-click once to increase the magnification

Using the Control Panel
Launch Print Preview. Then do one of the following:

Depending on the current level of magnification, one of the Zoom buttons may be greyed out, and therefore unavailable.

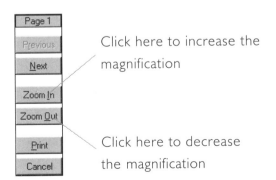

Click here to increase the magnification

Click here to decrease the magnification

Changing pages in Print Preview

Although you can only view one page at a time in Print Preview mode, you can step backwards and forwards through the database as often as necessary.

There are three methods you can use :

Using the Control Panel

Carry out the following actions:

 Depending on your location within the document (and the number of pages), one of these buttons may be greyed out, and therefore unavailable.

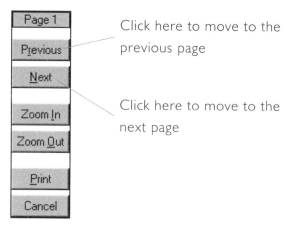

Click here to move to the previous page

Click here to move to the next page

Using the keyboard

 In a magnified page view, the Page Up and Page Down keys move through the current page.

You can use the following keyboard shortcuts:

Page Up	Moves to the previous page (but not within a magnified page view – see the HOT TIP)
Page Down	Moves to the next page (but not within a magnified page view – see the HOT TIP)
Up cursor	Within a magnified view of a page, moves towards the top of the page
Down cursor	Within a magnified view of a page, moves towards the base of the page

Using the scrollbars

When you're working with a magnified view of a page, use the vertical and/or horizontal scrollbars (using standard Windows techniques) to move up or down within the page.

Printing database data

When you print your data within List view, you can specify:

To print with the current Print dialog settings, ignore the procedures on pages 179-180. Instead, click this button in the Toolbar:

Printing begins at once.

- the number of copies you want printed

- whether you want the copies 'collated'. This is the process whereby Works 2000 prints one full copy at a time. For instance, if you're printing four copies of a 20-page database, Works prints pages 1-20 of the first copy, followed by pages 1-20 of the second and pages 1-20 of the third... And so on.

- which pages you want printed

- the printer you want to use (if you have more than one installed on your system)

You can 'mix and match' these, as appropriate.

Starting a print run

Open the database which contains the data you want to print. Pull down the File menu and click Print.

If this is the first time you've initiated a print-run in your current Works 2000 session, carry out steps 1-2 below, as appropriate (see the two HOT TIPS):

Re step 1 – if you click Quick tour of printing (for a guided tour explaining printing basics), follow the procedures in the two HOT TIPS on page 180. Then perform step 2 on the right, and steps 3-7 on page 180.

If, on the other hand, you select To print your document OR To print a specific page or range of pages in step 1, omit step 2 and simply carry out steps 3-7...

If you don't want to launch the printing guided tour or printing-specific assistance, omit step 1. Simply perform step 2, then steps 3-7 on page 180.

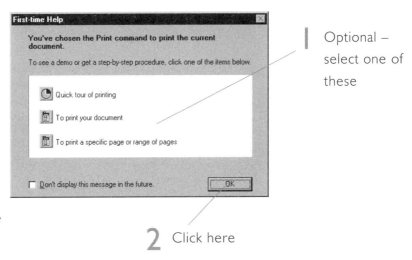

Optional – select one of these

2 Click here

To move through the tour, click either of these buttons:

 one screen back

 one screen on

If you followed step 1 on page 179, one of the following launches:

- a special tour relating to printing

- the Print dialog (plus on-screen help relating to printing)

- the Print dialog (plus help with printing page ranges)

To close the special tour at any time, click this button:

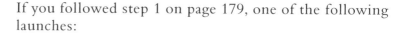

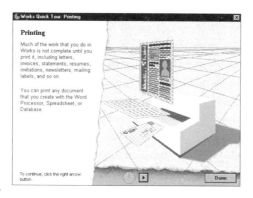

The first screen in the printing guided tour

If you launched the tour, follow the procedure in the HOT TIP above to close it before performing steps 2-7 on pages 179-180.

Follow steps 3-7 below, as appropriate:

3 Click here; select a printer from the list

If you're printing from within Form view, you have a further choice. Click Current record only to limit the print run to the active record.

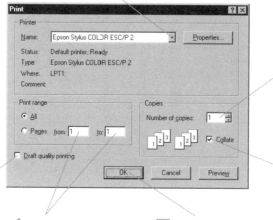

4 Type in the no. of copies required

5 Click here to turn collation on or off

Click Draft quality printing to have your database print with minimal formatting.

6 Type a page range

7 Click here

The Calendar

This chapter gives you the basics of using the Calendar. You'll learn how to view specific dates; switch to different views; and insert appointments and events. You'll go on to make appointments and events recurring, set alarms and apply filters as a way of restricting which appointments/ events display. Finally, you'll discover how to track national/religious holidays, and print out your Calendar.

Covers

The Calendar – an overview | 182

The Calendar screen | 183

Entering appointments | 184

Appointment management | 185

Entering events | 186

Chapter Five

The Calendar – an overview

To have Calendar display religious or national holidays, pull down the Edit menu and click Add Holidays. In the Add Holidays to Calendar dialog, select 1 or more countries. Click OK.

You can use the Calendar module to:

- track appointments

- track events

- track national holidays

- set alarms which remind you of important appointments/ events

- make appointments etc. recurring

Here, Week view is recording a UK holiday

Printing

To print the Calendar, pull down the File menu and click Print. Now do the following:

Click here; select a style

2 Specify a date range

3 If applicable, specify a time range

Re step 4 – select All appointments to print all appointments, OR Appointments currently selected in the Category Filter to print only pre-selected ones (see page 184).

4 Select one of these

5 Click here

6 Complete the 2nd Print dialog (for how to do this, see steps 3-6 on page 180) then click OK

The Calendar screen

Below is an illustration of the Calendar screen:

Here, the Calendar is displaying one day only, split into its component hours. This is called Day View.

(There are two other views. Week View shows a 7-day week, starting from Monday, while Month View shows every day in the given month.)

Title bar   Menu bar

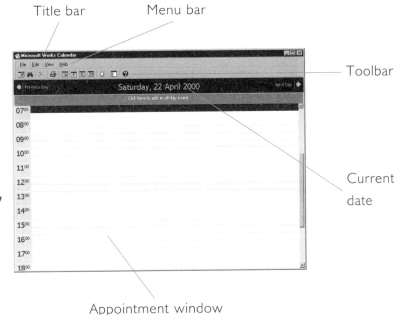

Toolbar

Current date

Appointment window

Re step 1 – you can also use an inbuilt calendar. Click the arrow to the right of the Enter date: field. Do the following:

Jumping to dates

To view new dates, pull down the Edit menu and click Go To, Date. (Alternatively, press Ctrl+G.) Now do the following:

A Click here to move back or forward a month

Enter a date

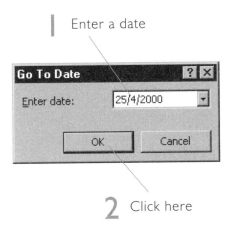

B Click here

Now perform step 2.

2 Click here

Entering appointments

In any Calendar view, double-click the day for which you want to enter the appointment. Do the following:

You can specify how many days the Calendar displays. Pull down the View menu and select Day, Week or Month.

To apply a category to your new appointment, click the Change button. In the dialog, select 1 or more categories. Click OK. Finally, perform step 5.

1 Name the appointment

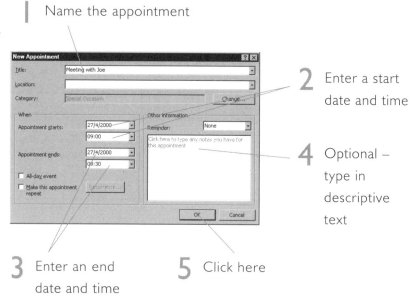

2 Enter a start date and time

4 Optional – type in descriptive text

3 Enter an end date and time

5 Click here

The Calendar lets you classify appointments. For example, if you apply a pre-defined category called 'Business' to all meetings you set up, you can have the Calendar display only those entries associated with the category. You do this by applying a filter.

Applying filters

Pull down the View menu and click Show Category Filter. Do the following:

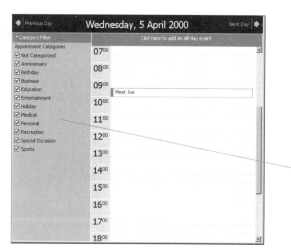

To view all appointments again, pull down the View menu and click Category Filter, Show appointments in all categories.

Deselect categories relating to appointments you don't want to view

Appointment management

To set up an alarm (either when you create an appointment, or when you edit it), click in this button:

In the list which launches, select a reminder option (e.g. '1 hour' or '1 week').

To make an appointment recurring (either when you create it or when you edit it), select Make this appointment repeat. Click this button:

Recurrence...

Complete the Recurrence Options dialog (e.g. specify the period you want the recurrence to operate, and the frequency). Click OK.

You can perform various actions on appointments you've already set up.

Editing appointments

In any Calendar view, double-click an appointment. Carry out steps 1–4, as appropriate. Finally, perform step 5:

1 Rename the appointment

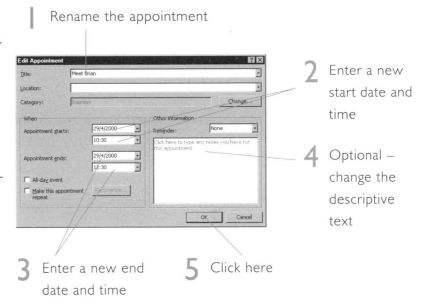

2 Enter a new start date and time

4 Optional – change the descriptive text

3 Enter a new end date and time

5 Click here

Moving appointments

First, launch the appropriate Calendar view. Place the mouse pointer over the relevant appointment. Hold down the left mouse button and drag it to a new date and/or time.

Deleting appointments

Right-click an appointment. In the menu, select Delete Item. Do the following:

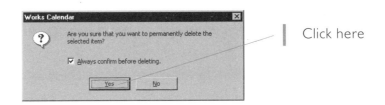

1 Click here

Entering events

The Calendar makes a distinction between appointments and events.

Appointments relate to a specific time (e.g. a meeting) while events either do not (e.g. a birthday) or are spread out over more than one day (e.g. holidays or conferences).

You can use the Calendar to track events – see the DON'T FORGET tip.

Creating an event

Select the relevant Calendar view and do the following:

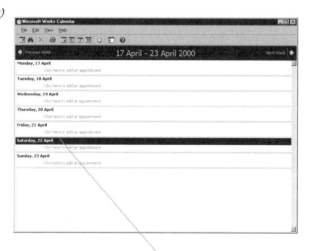

This is Week View. To select another view, see the HOT TIP on page 184.

To edit an existing event, double-click it in any view. Follow steps 1-5 (as appropriate) on page 185).

(Events can also be moved and deleted – follow the procedures under 'Moving appointments' and 'Deleting appointments' on page 185.)

1 Double-click the day you want the event to start on

2 Name the event   3 Enter a start date

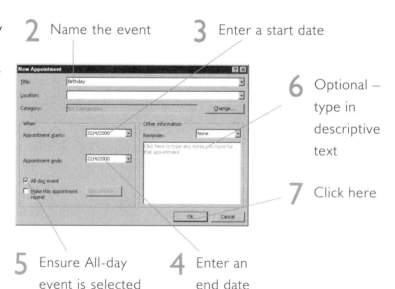

6 Optional – type in descriptive text

7 Click here

To make the event recurring, or to apply an alarm, follow the procedures in the two HOT TIPS on page 185.

5 Ensure All-day event is selected   4 Enter an end date

Index

A

Answer Wizard
  Using 23
Antonyms 61
Automatic word wrap 27
AVG function 159

C

Calendar 181–186
  Alarms
    Setting up 185–186
  An overview 182
  Appointments
    Deleting 185
    Editing 185
    Entering 184
    Making recurring 185
    Moving 185
  Categories
    Using 184
  Display
    Configuring 184
  Events
    Creating 186
    Deleting 186
    Making recurring 186
    Modifying 186
    Moving 186

Filters
  Applying 184
  Creating 184
  Removing 184
Printing 182
Screen components 183
Views
  Defined 183
  Switching between 184
Clip Gallery
  Categories
    Creating 72
    Renaming 73
  Clips
    Adding 76
    Adding from the Web 70
    Adding keywords to 74
    Deleting keywords in 74
    Finding by keywords 75
    Recategorising 70–71
  Closing 70
Creating blank documents 12

D

Database 143–180
  Arguments 157
  Best Fit
    Using 162
  Clip art
    Inserting 155
  Creating your first database 145
  Data
    Entering 146–147

Finding   169
Modifying   148
Printing   179–180
Replacing   170
Entry bar   147
Euro symbol
Inserting   147
Fields
Aligning   166
Bordering   167
Defined   145–146
Duplicating   163
Filling   163
Inserting   160
Selecting all   154
Shading   168
Wrapping text in   166
Fill series
Creating   164
Fonts/styles
Amending   165
Formulas
An overview   156
Inserting   157
Functions
AVG   159
Getting help with   158
Inserting   159
NOW()   156
Go To dialog
Using   152
Moving around in   151–152
Page setup
An overview   171
Gridlines   174
Margins   173
Page options   172
Record/field headings   174
Print Preview
Changing pages   178
Control Panel   178
Launching   176

Using Zoom in   177
Record/field size
Amending   162
Records
Defined   146
Filtering   163
Hiding   161
Inserting   161
Revealing   161
Sorting   162
Unfiltering   163
Reports
Creating   175
Defined   175
Viewing   176
Screen components   144
Selection Mode
Entering   154
Leaving   154
Selection techniques
In forms   155
in List view   154
Spell-checking   164
Toolbar
Displaying   144
Hiding   144
Views
Form   149
Form Design   149
List   149
Switching between   150
Zoom
Using   153
Zoom Area
Illustrated   144
Using   153
Database screen   9
Documents
Creating   12
From your templates   16
Via Wizards   13–14
Opening   17–18

In external formats   18
Saving
    As a template   15
    For the first time   19
    If previously saved   19
    In external formats   19
Sending by email   20

Images
    Bitmap   62
    Vector   62
Importing. *See* Documents: Opening: In
    external formats
Internet
    Downloading clips from   70

E

Easy Calc   110
Edit Mode   99
Emailing documents   20
Euro symbol
    Inserting   30, 97, 147
Exporting. *See* Documents: Saving: In
    external formats

L

Leading   43

H

N

HELP
    Answer Wizard
        Closing   23
        Using   23
    Contents   21
        Using with functions   158
    Help boxes   24
    Index
        Using   22
    Links
        Using   23
Horizontal scrollbar   8

New documents
    Creating   11
Non-breaking hyphens   30–31
NOW() function   156

P

Paragraph marks   30–31

S

Spreadsheet   95–142
  Arguments   108, 110
  AutoFill   116
  AutoFormat   125
  Basic data types   97
  Best Fit feature   113
  Cell alignment   121
    Customising   122
  Cell borders
    Applying   123
    Removing   123
  Cell ranges
    Jumping to   102
    Naming   100
  Cells
    Defined   97
    Filling   115
    Protecting   111–112
    Selecting all   106
    Unlocking   111
    Unprotecting   112
  Charts
    Amending formats   130
    Creating   129
    Data series defined   131
    Deleting   132
    Fine-tuning   129
    Previewing in situ   138
    Reformatting   131
    Viewing   132
  Column width
    Changing   113
  Columns
    Inserting   114
    Selecting   106

Data
  Amending   99
  Entering   97–98
  Finding   126
  Printing   141–142
  Replacing   127
Edit Mode   99
Euro symbol
  Inserting   97
Fast-track printing   142
Fonts/styles
  Changing   120
Footers
  Inserting   118
  Viewing   118
Formulas
  Entering   108
  Viewing   109
Functions   109
Headers
  Editing   117
  Inserting   117
  Viewing   117
Moving around in   101
Number formats
  Applying   119
Page setup
  An overview   133
  Charts   137
  Gridlines   136
  Margin options   135
  Page options   134
Patterns
  Applying   124
Print Preview   117–118
  Changing pages   140
  Launching   138
  Using Zoom in   139
Ranges
  Selecting   105
Row height
  Changing   113

Rows
    Inserting   114
    Selecting   106
Screen components   96
Spell-checking   99
Text wrap   122
Titles
    Freezing   99
    Unfreezing   99
Undo   125
Zoom
    Using   103
Zoom Area   96
Spreadsheet screen   9

Tabs   48–49
Task Launcher   11
    History section
        Using   17
    Programs section
        Using   13, 145
        Running automatically   12
    Tasks section
        Using   12–13, 16
Templates   11
    Saving your work as   15
    Using   16
Title bar   8
Toolbars   8
    Hiding/revealing   10
ToolTips   24

Vertical scrollbar   8

Windows Startup menu   17
Wizards   11
    Using   13–14
Word Processor   25–94
    Automatic word wrap   27
    Borders
        Applying   46
    Character formatting   34
    Columns
        Applying   45
    Endnotes
        Creating   29
        Finding   29
    Euro symbol
        Inserting   30
    Fills
        Applying   47
    Find-and-replace operations   51
    Font effects
        Applying   38
    Font styles
        Applying   37
    Footers
        Amending   55
        Described   52
        Inserting   54
    Footnotes
        Creating   29

Finding   29
Grammar-checking
   Running   60
   Turning off   60
Headers
   Amending   55
   Described   52
   Inserting   53
Images
   Adding to the Clip Gallery   76
   An overview   64–65
   Bordering   80
   Inserting as clip art   66–67
   Inserting as pictures   68–69
   Moving   81
   Rescaling   78–79
   Selecting   77
   Wrapping text around   82–83
Line spacing
   Changing   43
Manual hyphens
   Inserting   31
Margins
   Customising   85
Moving around in   28
Page orientation   86
Page setup   84
Page sizes
   Setting   87
Paragraph formatting   34
Paragraph spacing
   Applying   42
Print Preview   93
   Caveats   88
   Changing pages in   90
   Launching   88
   Toolbar   89
   Zooming in and out in   89
Printer setup   91
Printing
   An overview   92
   Customising   93

Fast-track   94
   To a file   93
Redo   57
Screen components
   Customising   26
Special characters
   Inserting   31
   Searching for   50
   Viewing   30
Spell-checking
   On-the-fly   58
   Separately   59
Synonyms and antonyms   61
Tab stops
   Setting   48–49
Text
   Aligning   41
   Entering   27
   Indenting   39
   Wrapping around images   82
Text colour
   Changing   36
Text searches   50
Text wrap
   Applying to images   83
Thesaurus   61
Type sizes
   Applying   35
Typefaces
   Applying   35
Undo   56
Word count
   Performing   27
Zoom levels
   Setting   32